New Century College English Course (2)

新世纪英语教程学习指导 ②

主　编　刘世伟
副主编　李丽莎　唐树良

图书在版编目(CIP)数据

新世纪英语教程学习指导.2/刘世伟主编.—北京:北京大学出版社,2005.10
(全国高职高专公共英语教材)
ISBN 978-7-301-09057-2

Ⅰ.新… Ⅱ.刘… Ⅲ.英语－高等学校:技术学校－教学参考资料 Ⅳ.H31

中国版本图书馆 CIP 数据核字(2005)第 065426 号

"十一五"国家重点图书出版规划
湖南省教育科学"十一五"规划重点课题

书　　　　名:	新世纪英语教程学习指导(2)
著作责任者:	刘世伟　主编
责 任 编 辑:	黄瑞明
标 准 书 号:	ISBN 978-7-301-09057-2/H·1486
出 版 发 行:	北京大学出版社
地　　　　址:	北京市海淀区成府路 205 号　100871
网　　　　址:	http://www.pup.cn
电　　　　话:	邮购部 62752015　发行部 62750672　编辑部 62767347　出版部 62754962
电 子 邮 箱:	zbing@pup.pku.edu.cn
印　刷　者:	北京宏伟双华印刷有限公司
经　销　者:	新华书店
	787毫米×1092毫米　16 开本　9.75 印张　240 千字
	2005 年 10 月第 1 版　2007 年 12 月第 2 次印刷
定　　　价:	12.00 元

未经许可,不得以任何方式复制或抄袭本书之部分或全部内容。
版权所有,侵权必究　举报电话:010-62752024
　　　　　　　　　　电子邮箱:fd@pup.pku.edu.cn

前　言

　　《新世纪英语教程学习指导》第二册在全国高校素质教育教材研究与编写委员会支持下，由高职高专英语教材编写组编写；湖南网络工程职业学院刘世伟为主编，湖南广播电视大学李丽莎、保定金融高等专科学校唐树良为副主编。供招收高中毕业生、中专毕业生和职高毕业生的三年制高等职业学院和高等普通专科学校的学生以及英语自学者使用。

　　本教材按照教育部高等教育司《高职高专教育英语课程教学基本要求》编写，要求学生在学习本教材前，应掌握《新世纪英语教程》第一册的语音、词汇和语法知识，在听、说、读、写、译等方面具备一定的基础。

　　本教材贯彻听说领先的原则，重在培养学生实际使用英语进行交际的能力，同时培养学生较强的阅读能力，并兼顾写作、翻译等各项能力的发展，使学生具备以英语为工具，捕捉和获取所需信息的能力，为学习各种专业英语打下坚实基础。

　　本教材共分四册，语言材料大部分选自原文材料，具有较强的思想性、科学性、知识性、趣味性和实用性。第一、二册的内容以共核英语语言(Common Core English)为主，第三、四册适当增加科普内容的比例。学生学完第三册后可以达到《高职高专教育英语课程教学基本要求》所规定的B级要求，学完第四册后可以达到《高职高专教育英语课程教学基本要求》所规定的A级要求。

　　第一、二册的编排体例采用主题教学(Theme-based)模式：从不同侧面围绕一个激发学生兴趣和思考的共同主题，把听、说、读、写、译等各种技能的训练合理安排在一个单元内，教学活动以阅读为中心，结合主题预演、课文问答、语言结构、听力理解、交际技巧、翻译训练、应用写作等，从而将教与学有机结合，课内外连成一片，使学生真正做到听得懂、说得出、用得活。

　　本册有8个单元，每单元有80～100个词汇，15～25个短语，每单元包括课文选读(分为Text A和Text B)和课文理解、语言结构和练习、实践与提高三个部分。课文选读有两篇内容相关、语言结构相同的课文，为语言结构和练习及实践与提高提供了听、说、读、写、译各项练习的中心材料，语言结构和练习及实践与提高则围绕课文材料紧密进行。每个单元的语言结构和练习着重讲清并解决一个语法方面的难题。实践与提高则强调对听、说、读、写、译各种技能的培养，其中阅读技巧有与课文选读内容相关、语言结构相似的三篇材料，前两篇为快速阅读，后一篇为完型填空，内容与课文相近但难度稍浅，旨在培养学生快速获取信息的能力；听力技巧有辨音、对话和填空等练习，旨在培养学生的听力理解能力；交际技巧以诗歌朗读作为热身练习，过渡到日常会话，重在培养学生的交际能力；翻译技巧主要是语言结构和短语、习语的练习；写作技巧从课文选读重点句型的模仿入手，重在掌握日常应用文的写作。每单元提供的练习形式多且数量大，教师可根据教学的实际情况进行取舍。

　　《新世纪英语教程学习指导》每单元的内容包括教学目的、词语运用、练习答案、听力理解的磁带原文和参考译文五个部分，此外每个单元后面还附有网上资源，供教师备课参考，学有余力的学生也可在课后上网学习。书中给出了期中复习测试和期末复习测试的参考答案，书后还附有教学大纲和实施方案，希望能对学生学习和教师备课有所帮助。

本教材的教学课时建议为72课时,每个单元的教学课时为8课时,另外每4个单元后有一个复习材料,每个复习材料的教学课时为4课时。

本书承英国文化教育委员会理事、英国东伦敦大学语言中心高级讲师Amanda Maitland女士,美国阿拉巴马州立大学教育学院Louise Lee博士审阅并提出宝贵修改意见,在此一并表示感谢。

由于时间仓促,书中疏漏之处在所难免,请读者与专家指正。

高职高专英语教材编写组
2005年8月

CONTENTS

Unit One — Birds Finding Their Way Home

The Things Unknown to You	**1**
Objective	1
Word Usage	2
Key to Unit 1	10
Tape Scripts for Listening Comprehension	15
Text Translation for Reference	17

Unit Two — Precautions against SARS

Fight against AIDS	**20**
Objective	20
Word Usage	21
Key to Unit 2	29
Tape Scripts for Listening Comprehension	34
Text Translation for Reference	36

Unit Three — Qinshan Nuclear Power Station

Energy Sense Makes Future Sense	**39**
Objective	39
Word Usage	40
Key to Unit 3	47
Tape Scripts for Listening Comprehension	52
Text Translation for Reference	54

Unit Four — Can Human Beings Be Cloned?

The Cloning Technology	**57**
Objective	57
Word Usage	58
Key to Unit 4	64
Tape Scripts for Listening Comprehension	69
Text Translation for Reference	71

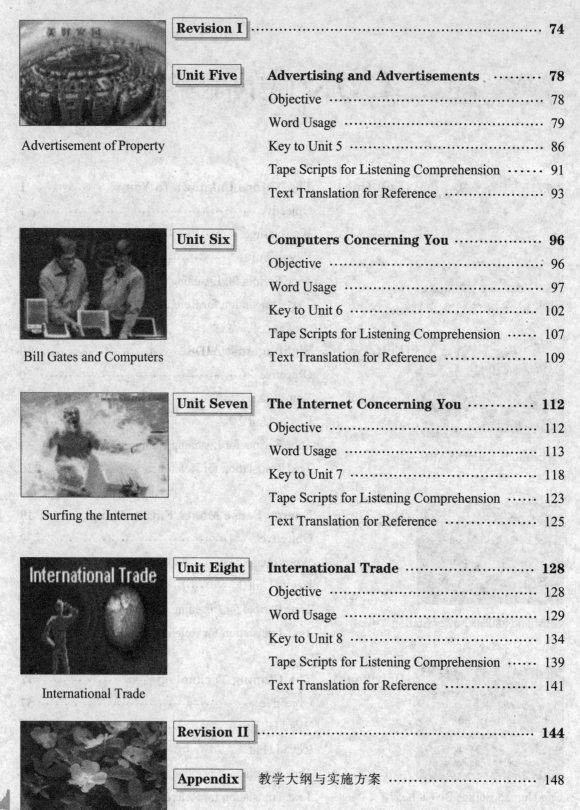

	Revision I	74
Advertisement of Property	**Unit Five** Advertising and Advertisements	78
	Objective	78
	Word Usage	79
	Key to Unit 5	86
	Tape Scripts for Listening Comprehension	91
	Text Translation for Reference	93
Bill Gates and Computers	**Unit Six** Computers Concerning You	96
	Objective	96
	Word Usage	97
	Key to Unit 6	102
	Tape Scripts for Listening Comprehension	107
	Text Translation for Reference	109
Surfing the Internet	**Unit Seven** The Internet Concerning You	112
	Objective	112
	Word Usage	113
	Key to Unit 7	118
	Tape Scripts for Listening Comprehension	123
	Text Translation for Reference	125
International Trade	**Unit Eight** International Trade	128
	Objective	128
	Word Usage	129
	Key to Unit 8	134
	Tape Scripts for Listening Comprehension	139
	Text Translation for Reference	141
Beautiful Wild Flowers	**Revision II**	144
	Appendix 教学大纲与实施方案	148

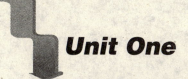

Unit One

THE THINGS UNKNOWN TO YOU

Objective

By the end of this unit, the learners are required to grasp the following:

I. Key Words and Phrases

   1. Words:

ability	blindfold	compass	confuse	direction
mysterious	nest	prove	sense	researcher

   2. Phrases:

a wide range of	be born with	catch on
compare... to	decide on	have some difficulty (in)
make researches on	set free	turn out

   Also: compare... with

II. Language Structure

   The Use of "It"

III. Practice and Improvement

   Reading Skills: Speed Reading and Cloze Procedure
   Speaking Skills: Making Telephone Calls
   Listening Skills: Sentence Judgment, Dialogues, and Spot Dictation
   Translation Skills: Phrases and the Use of "It"
   Writing Skills: Sentence Patterns and Envelopes

Word Usage

Reading Selection

Text A

1) It's known to all that home pigeons are intelligent birds, **considering** that a 1-pound bundle of feathers has better **navigational** equipment in it than the newest jet plane.

   considering *prep. & conj.* used for saying that you have a particular opinion about something, because of a particular fact about it 考虑到,就……来说

   e.g. *Considering she'd only been there once before, she did well to find the way.*
       她仅仅去过那儿一次就找到了路,表现已经很不错了。
       It is still in excellent condition considering that it was built 600 years ago.
       就其600年的建造历史而言,这个建筑物目前的状况仍然很完好。

   navigational *adj.* 航行的
   navigate *v.* sail over (a sea); sail up or down (a river) 航行于(海上),(沿河)上下游航行
   navigation *n.* [U] the act of navigating 航行

   e.g. navigational errors 航行(海)错误
       navigational equipment 航海设备
       Sailors have special equipment to help them navigate.
       海员用特殊的设备帮助他们航行。
       Even ancient ships were able to navigate large stretches of open water.
       即使是古老的船只也能在辽阔的水域航行。
       In the past, navigation depended on knowledge of the positions of the stars.
       过去,航行是靠着星星的方位来确定方向的。
       Mechanics discovered problems with the plane's navigation system.
       机械师发现飞机的航行系统出问题了。

2) There are a few **clues.**

   clue *n.* a sign or some information which helps you to find the answer to a problem, question or mystery 线索,暗示

   e.g. *Police are still looking for clues in their search for the missing girl.*
       警察一直都在寻找失踪女孩的线索。
       I'm never going to guess the answer if you don't give me a clue.
       如果你不给我提示,我是猜不到答案的。

3) It **proves** they don't **rely on** good eyesight to **decide on** a flight plan.

prove　*v.*　to show a particular result after a period of time　证实(是),证明

e.g.　The operation proved a complete success.
这次手术(证明)是极其成功的。

The dispute over the song rights proved impossible to resolve.
对这首歌的版权归属问题的争论是没法解决的。

The new treatment has proved to be a disaster.
新的疗法(证明)是很不成功的。

rely on sb/sth
① to need a particular thing or the help and support of someone or something in order to continue, to work correctly, or to succeed　依赖,依靠
② to trust someone or something or to expect them to behave in a particular way　指望

e.g.　The success of this project relies on everyone making an effort.
这个项目的成功靠的是大家的努力。

I rely on you for good advice.
我靠你出个好主意。

British weather can never be relied on—it's always changing.
英国的天气是靠不住的——它变化多端。

Don't rely on finding me here when you get back (= I might have gone).
你回来的时候别指望能找到我。

decide　*v.*　to choose something, especially after thinking carefully about several possibilities　决定

decide on sth/sb　to choose something or someone after careful thought　(经过考虑)做决定

e.g.　They have to decide by next Friday.
他们下周五以前必须做出决定。

In the end, we decided to go to the theatre.
最后我们决定去看电影。

He can't decide whether to buy it.
他不能决定是否买下。

I've decided on blue for the bathroom.
我决定把浴室装修成蓝色的。

He has not decided on his course yet.
他还没决定修哪门课程。

4) The **entire** world is covered with a magnetic field.

entire　*adj.*　whole or complete, with nothing missing　完全的,全部的

entirely　*adv.*　completely　全部

e.g. *He'd spent the entire journey asleep.*
整个旅途中他都在睡觉。

I admit it was entirely my fault.
我承认这都是我的错。

The company is run almost entirely by middle-aged men.
这个公司几乎是清一色的中年人。

5) The North Pole **attracts** magnetic material, like compass needles...

attract   *v.*   (of people, things, places, etc.) to pull or draw someone or something towards them by the qualities they have, especially positive and admirable ones   吸引，引起注意

attraction   *n.*   [C or U] something which makes people want to go to a place or do a particular thing   吸引人的东西，吸引力

attractive   *adj.*   very pleasing in appearance or sound, or causing interest or pleasure   吸引人的，招人喜爱的

e.g. *These flowers are brightly colored in order to attract butterflies.*
这些花争奇斗艳，吸引着许多的蝴蝶。

Her ideas have attracted a lot of attention in the scientific community.
她的观点引起了科学界的注意。

I'm not attracted to him.
我没有引起他的注意。

Life in London has so many attractions—nightclubs, good restaurants and so on.
伦敦的生活有许多吸引人的地方——夜总会、高级饭店等等。

Skiing holds no attraction for me.
滑雪对我来说没有吸引力。

She is a very attractive young woman.
她是一个非常招人喜欢的年轻女人。

6) A pigeon might feel a pull toward north in its neck and **compare** it **with** its own coop.

compare... with   to examine or look for the difference between two or more things   与……比较

compare... to   to judge, suggest or consider that something is similar or of equal quality to something else   把……比作

e.g. *Children seem to learn more interesting things compared with when we were at school.*
现在小孩在学校学的东西与我们那时相比有趣一些。

The hotel certainly compared favorably with the one we stayed in last year.
这家酒店与我们去年住的那家酒店相比要好。

Still only twenty-five, she has been compared to the greatest dancer of all time.
刚刚25岁的她就被当作了最了不起的舞蹈家。

7) However, it seems clear that more than magnetism **is involved.**

    involve   *v.*   to include someone or something in something, or to make them take part in or feel part of it   涉及；包括

    e.g.   The second accident involved two cars and a lorry.
           第二起车祸涉及(殃及)两辆小轿车和一辆货车。
           The operation involves putting a small tube into your heart.
           这次手术就是(包括)在你的心脏里放一根细小的管子。
           It would be difficult not to involve the child's father in the arrangements.
           不把这孩子的父亲安排进来是很困难的。

8) If the pigeons **had been directed** only by the magnetism of the earth, they would have been confused.

    direct
    ① *adj.*   straight   直接的
    ② *adj.*   describes someone who says what they think in a very honest way without worrying about other people's opinions   直率的
    ③ *v.*   to tell someone how to get somewhere   指路
    ④ *v.*   to control or be in charge of an activity, organization, etc.   指导

    direction   *n.*   [U] control or instruction   指导
    directly   *adv.*   very soon; immediately   迅速，马上
                  conj.   immediately after; as soon as   即刻

    e.g.   Is there a direct train to Edinburgh?
           有到爱丁堡的直达车吗？
           She decided to take direct control of the project.
           她决定直接控制这个项目。
           Have you any direct experience of this kind of work?
           对于这种工作你有直接的经验吗？
           There is a direct connection between smoking and lung cancer.
           吸烟与肺癌之间有着直接的关联。
           I like her open and direct manner.
           我喜欢她开朗和率直的性格。
           Could you direct me to the airport?
           你能告诉我怎么去飞机场吗？
           I couldn't find the station, so I asked someone if they could direct me.
           我找不着车站，于是我问别人能否给我指路。
           There was a police officer directing the traffic.
           有一名警察在指挥交通。
           The project was under the direction of a well-known academic.
           这一项目由一位著名学者指导。

When you get home you're going directly to bed.
到家了就马上上床休息。
Directly he was paid, he went out shopping.
他一拿到报酬,就出去购物了。
I'll be with you directly I've finished this letter.
写完信,我马上和你在一起。

9) It's **mysterious** how homing pigeons use all these senses.
   mystery *n.* something strange or unknown which has not yet been explained or understood
      神秘,奥秘;神秘的事
   mysterious *adj.* 神秘的
   mysteriously *adv.* 神秘地
   e.g. *The book tries to explain some of the mysteries of life.*
      这本书力图解释生活中的一些神秘的事情。
   It's a complete mystery to me why (= I do not understand why) she married him at all!
   她竟然和他结婚,这对我来说,完全就是个谜。
   He died in mysterious circumstances, and there is still a possibility that it was murder.
   他死得那么蹊跷,仍有可能是谋杀。
   Mysteriously, the light came on, although no one was near the switch.
   神了,没人走近开关,灯却亮了。

10) Other tests have shown that pigeons can **detect** tiny changes in the gravity of the earth.
   detect *v.* to notice something that is partly hidden or not clear or to discover something, especially using a special method   察觉,侦查,探测
   detection *n.* [U] when someone notices or discovers something   发觉
   detective *n.* someone whose job is to discover information about crimes and find out who is responsible for them   侦探
   e.g. *Some sounds cannot be detected by the human ear.*
   有些声音是人类察觉不到的。
   Financial experts have detected signs that the economy is beginning to improve.
   财经专家已经察觉到经济状况开始有所改进。
   High levels of lead were detected in the atmosphere.
   空气中被测到含铅量过高。
   Radar equipment is used to detect (= find the position of) enemy aircraft.
   雷达是用来探测敌方的飞机的。
   Early detection of the cancer improves the chances of successful treatment.
   癌症早发现有助于增加病人治愈的机会。
   He is a private detective.
   他是个私家侦探。

These are detective stories.
这些都是侦探小说。

11) Do they **figure out** the angle of the sun?
   figure *v.* to calculate an amount 计算
   figure out to finally understand something or someone, or find the solution to a problem after a lot of thought 想出,弄清,算出
   e.g. *I'm still figuring my taxes.*
   我还在计算我的税额呢。
   I can't figure out why he did it.
   我弄不明白他为什么这么做。
   Can you figure out the answer to question 5?
   你能想出第五个问题的答案吗?

Outline:

I. (Para. 1) Introduction
Homing pigeons are very intelligent birds.

II. (Para. 2–6)
There are some clues that homing pigeons can find their way home, even if they are taken to a strange place.
1. Homing pigeons don't rely on good eyesight to decide on a flight plan. (Para. 2)
2. Magnetism may be part of the answer. (Para. 3)
3. It is possible for them to navigate by the sun and the magnetism. (Para. 4–5)
4. There are more possibilities. (Para. 6)

III. (Para. 7–8) Conclusion
It is a mystery how homing pigeons use all these senses, and it is far from being settled.

Text B

1) Scientists who try to **predict** earthquakes have got some new assistants recently—animals.
   predict *v.* to say that an event or action will happen in the future, especially as a result of knowledge or experience 预言,预示
   e.g. *It's still not possible to accurately predict the occurrence of earthquakes.*
   要准确地预测地震的发生仍然不太可能。
   Who could have predicted that within ten years he'd be in charge of the whole company?
   谁又能预言十年后他全权负责公司呢?

No one can predict when the disease will strike again.
谁也不能预告这场疾病什么时候再次爆发。

2) Scientists have begun to **catch on** what farmers have known for thousands of years.

   catch on   to understand, especially after a long time   理会,明白

   e.g.   *Jack is always the last to catch on my joke.*
   杰克总是最后一个弄明白我的笑话。
   Would you mind repeating what you said? I didn't catch on.
   你能把你所说的再重复一遍吗？我没听明白。

3) Animals often seem to know **in advance** that an earthquake is coming, and they show their fear by acting in strange ways.

   in advance   before a particular time, or before doing a particular thing   预先,事先

   e.g.   *If you're going to come, please let me know in advance.*
   如果你要来,请事先通知我。
   Everything is fixed in advance.
   一切都预先安排好了。

4) It's also difficult **at times** to tell the difference between normal animal **restlessness** and "earthquake nerves."

   at times   sometimes   有时

   e.g.   *You can be really annoying at times, you know.*
   你知道,有时你真的很烦人。
   I do feel a little nervous at times.
   有时我真的感到有些紧张。

   rest   *v.*   to be still or quiet; to be free from activity   平静,宁静

   restless   *adj.*   unwilling or unable to stay still or to be quiet and calm, because you are worried or bored   不能平静的,不安的

   restlessly   *adv.*   焦躁不安地

   restlessness   *n.*   [U]   焦躁不安

   e.g.   *The doctor told him that he should rest for a few days.*
   医生告诉他应该休息几天。
   He looked away from the computer screen to rest his eyes.
   为了让自己的眼睛得到休息,他没一直盯着电脑看。
   He's a restless type—he never stays in one country for long.
   他属于不安定的那一类——他绝不会在一个国家呆很长时间。
   She spent a restless night (= She did not sleep well).
   她度过了一个不眠之夜。

She shifted restlessly in her chair.
她焦躁不安地在椅子上摇动。

He was seized with a restlessness he could not account for.
他突然感到一阵莫明奇妙的不安情绪。

5) It **turned out** that the puma had an upset stomach.
   turn out   happen to be   结果是……
   turn sth out   to produce or make something, often quickly or in large amounts   生产，制造
   e.g.   *The truth turned out to be stranger than we had expected.*
   事实比我们所想到的要怪得多。
   It turns out that she had known him when they were children.
   结果是，还在孩提时，她就认识他了。
   They turn out thousands of these games every week.
   他们每周都会推出多种游戏。

6) They were **shut up** in an area that was being shaken by a series of tiny earthquakes.
   shut (sth) up   to close a shop or other business for a period of time, usually when business is finished for the day   关门，停止营业
   shut sb/sth up   to keep a person or animal in an enclosed place   密封，封闭
   shut (sb) up   stop talking   住口
   e.g.   *By the time we got there, all the market traders were shutting up.*
   我们到那儿时，所有的店铺都关门了。
   My dad never stops talking. It's impossible to shut him up!
   我父亲总是不停地说，很难让他住口。
   She can't spend her whole life shut up in her office.
   她不能老把自己封闭在办公室。
   I wish you'd shut up for a moment and listen to what the rest of us have to say.
   我真希望你能停一会儿，听听我们其他人的说法。

Outline:

I. (Para. 1–2) Introduction

Scientists have got some animals to predict earthquakes.

II. (Para. 3–6)

Animals often seem to know in advance that an earthquake is coming.

1. They show their fear by acting in strange ways before an earthquake. (Para. 3)
2. Which types of animal behaviors predict earthquakes? (Para. 4)
3. What kind of warnings do the animals receive? And there's a good example occurred with a group of dogs. (Para. 5–6)

III. (Para. 7) Conclusion

It's a job for future scientists to discover what animals can sense and to learn how they know it is a danger signal.

Key to Unit 1

Exercises for Reading Comprehension

I. **Answer the following questions.**
1. Yes, I do. It is because a pigeon seems to have better navigational equipment in it than the newest jet plane.
2. No, it doesn't.
3. Yes, they could.
4. The North Pole attracts magnetic material, and the South Pole repels magnetic material.
5. It is a device with a needle that points north.
6. With the tiny pieces of magnetic material in the neck muscles, a pigeon might feel a pull toward north in its neck and compare it with its own coop, and the difference in pull could tell it which direction to find.
7. If it was a cloudy day, the pigeons that flew got lost.
8. Researchers in Italy plugged the nostrils of some pigeons and then set them free. The birds had some difficulty in getting home, which suggests that smell might be involved.
9. The pigeons can also sense a much wider range of light and sound than people can.
10. It is mysterious how homing pigeons use all these senses. Are they born with a magnetic map of the earth? Do they figure out the angle of the sun? How do they make a map out of the sights, smells and sounds they receive? And finally, where in those little birds' brains is all that knowledge kept?
11. It is animals that help scientists to predict earthquakes.
12. Yes, they have.
13. Animals often seem to know in advance that an earthquake is coming, and they show their fear by acting in strange ways. For example, before a Chinese earthquake in 1975, snakes awoke from their winter sleep early only to freeze to death in the cold air; cows broke their halters and tried to escape; chickens refused to enter their coops.
14. No, I don't think so because it's difficult at times to tell the difference between normal animal restlessness and "earthquake nerves."
15. A zoo keeper once called earthquake researchers to say that his puma had been acting strangely.
16. No, it wasn't. It turned out that the puma had an upset stomach!

17. It is because that some animals can detect some tiny change in gravity or the magnetism of the earth while people hear and feel nothing.
18. Because they were reacting to the booming noise.
19. Yes, they can.
20. It is a job for future scientists to discover what animals can sense and to learn how they know it is a danger signal.

II. Find words in the text which mean approximately the same as the following, using the given letter as a clue.
1. attract
2. blindfold
3. confuse
4. detect
5. earthquake
6. involve
7. mystery
8. navigate
9. predict
10. restlessness

III. Complete the sentences with the given expressions, and change the form where necessary.
1. a wide range of
2. decided on
3. had some difficulty (in)
4. turned out
5. compare... with
5. compare... to
7. were set free
8. catch on
9. are born with
10. had been making researches on

IV. Complete the following passage by using appropriate words listed below, and be sure to use the correct forms for verbs and proper singular or plural forms for nouns.
1. sense
2. nests
3. proved
4. ability
5. researchers
6. blindfolded
7. confusing
8. direction
9. mysterious
10. compass

Exercises for Language Structure

I. Point out the use of "it" in the following sentences and then put them into Chinese.
1. However, it seems clear that more than magnetism is involved.
然而,看起来很清楚所涉及的远非只是磁力。(先行词 it 作形式主语)
2. If it was a cloudy day, the pigeon that flew got lost.
如果是阴天,飞行的鸽子就会迷路。(代词 it 表示天气)

3. It's also necessary for scientists to find out exactly what kind of warnings the animals receive.

   科学家也有必要准确地查明动物所接受的是哪种预兆。(先行词 it 作形式主语)

4. Scientists consider it possible that this sense helps animals to predict earthquakes.

   科学家认为这种感觉有可能帮助动物预报地震。(先行词 it 作形式宾语)

5. It is sunny today. But it is said that it is going to rain tomorrow. How changeable it is in spring!

   今天天晴,但据说明天将要下雨,春天的天气真是变化无常!(第一个 it 是代词,表示天气;第二个 it 是先行词,作形式主语;第三个 it 是代词,表示天气)

6. It was not until he entered a middle school that he began learning English.

   他是在进入中学后,才开始学习英语的。(It 构成断裂句,用来强调状语,本身无词义)

7. It's no more mysterious why animals can help us to predict earthquakes.

   为什么动物能帮助我们预报地震已经不再神秘了。(先行词 it 作形式主语)

8. It turns out that the children in the countryside have more difficulty in learning English than those in the city.

   原来是乡村的孩子比城里的孩子在学习英语方面存在更多的困难。(先行词 it 作形式主语)

9. This radio isn't mine; it's hers.

   这台收音机不是我的,而是她的。(代词 it 代替前面的指示代词 This)

10. Scientists still find it difficult to work out the mystery.

    科学家发现仍然很难解开这道谜。(先行词 it 作形式宾语)

II. Choose the best answer.

1. B 2. C 3. C 4. D 5. B 6. A 7. A 8. D 9. C 10. C

III. Find out which of the underlined parts in each sentence is not correct in written English.

1. B. when 改为 that
2. C. watching 改为 to watch
3. B. that 改为 it
4. C. this 改为 it
5. B. where 改为 that
6. C. him who 改为 he who/that
7. C. when 改为 that
8. B. which 改为 that
9. C. to regret 改为 regretting
10. B. for you to tell 改为 your telling

Practice and Improvement

Reading Skills

Speed Reading I

1. D 2. B 3. D 4. D 5. D 6. T 7. T 8. F 9. F 10. T

Speed Reading II

1. B 2. C 3. D 4. C 5. B 6. F 7. F 8. T 9. T 10. T

Cloze Procedure

1. A 2. A 3. D 4. B 5. D 6. D 7. A 8. C 9. D 10. A

Communication Function

II. Conversation

Calling for a Taxi

A: Hello.
B: Is that 2256708?
A: Yes, this is the Taxi Service Center. Can I help you?
B: Oh, I'm Greg Cook from Hunan Polytechnic of Network Engineering. Could you send a taxi, please?
A: What's your address?
B: Hunan Polytechnic of Network Engineering, 168 Qingyuan Road.
A: Where would you like to go?
B: Oh, to the Huanghua Airport.
B: Certainly. When will you need the taxi?
A: As soon as possible, please.
B: Okay, I'll page for the nearest taxi to your address.
A: I'll wait at the front gate. Thank you.
B: My pleasure. Good-bye.
A: Good-bye.

Listening Comprehension

I. 1. A 2. C 3. C 4. C 5. B 6. A 7. D 8. C 9. D 10. C

II. 1. D 2. C 3. A 4. C 5. B 6. A 7. B 8. C 9. D 10. D

III. 1. Despite   2. unknown
     3. fly over   4. by saying
     5. a sense of direction   6. an instinct
     7. explain   8. to gain food
     9. signals   10. a mystery

Translation Skills

I. Translate the following into English.

1. It remains mysterious how homing pigeons decide on their flight route by relying on their various senses.
2. The result of the exam shows that he still has some difficulty in learning English.
3. As a foreigner, Mr. Brown can't catch on what the sentence exactly means.
4. It turned out that he had learned what the report involved in advance.
5. Having made a series of operations, he figured out the difficult mathematical problem.

II. Translate the following into Chinese.

1. 信鸽如何依赖各种感官来决定其飞行路线仍然是一个谜。
2. 原来整个地球被磁场覆盖着,北极吸引磁性物体,南极排斥磁性物体。
3. 教我们磁学的正是李教授。
4. 他们是在两年后生产出这种监测器的。
5. 科学家认为目前不可能解开这道谜。

Writing Skills

I. Rewrite each of the sentences after the models.

Model A:

1. It is known by many people that several small earthquakes often come before or after a large one.
2. It is not without difficulty for the pigeons with their nostrils plugged to fly home.
3. It is a serious problem how to predict an earthquake.
4. It is known after the experiment whether the end of the magnet will attract or repel magnetic material.
5. It is quite difficult getting everything ready in time.

Model B:

1. It was homing pigeons that people began to use to send messages.
2. It is on rotating tables that the homing pigeons have been placed to confuse their sense of direction.
3. It was an Arabian horse that became very nervous and tried to break out of its stall.
4. It was in December, 2003 that an earthquake occurred in Iran.
5. It was earthquake researchers that a zoo keeper once called to say that his puma had been acting strangely.

II. Practical Writing

Wang Haihong
Sales Manager
Hunan Import and Export Corp.
68 May 1 East Road, Changsha
Hunan, 410007
P.R.China

Stamp

Confidential

Mr. Edward Green
Import Manager
Galaxy Trade Co., 165 Seaside Drive
Liverpool, SD1 5LV
United Kingdom

Tape Scripts for Listening Comprehension

I. Directions: *In this section you will hear 10 statements. Each statement will be read only once. Then there will be a pause. During the pause, you must read the four choices marked A, B, C and D, and decide which is closest in meaning to the sentence you have just heard, and then choose the corresponding letter.*

1. John can't keep a secret.
2. Mr. Brown doesn't have a car and neither do Tom and Nancy.
3. The apples cost 60 cents a pound, and I bought three pounds.
4. Any time he calls, I pretend I am out.
5. They have three bottles of milk, but they want two more.
6. Sarah was supposed to come at 7:00, but the time was half an hour early.
7. When we finish the class, we will make an experiment.
8. Flight 14 to Washington leaves at 8: 40.
9. I'd better see if Joe can help me with my report.
10. Our club meets every other Friday.

II. Directions: *In this section, you will hear 10 short conversations. At the end of each conversation, a question will be asked about what was said. The conversation and the question will be spoken only one time. After each question, there will be a pause. During the pause, you must read the four choices marked A, B, C and D, and decide which the best answer is, and then choose the corresponding letter.*

1. W: Did you study for the exam?
   M: I couldn't. I lent my notes to someone in the class.
   Q: What happened to the man?

2. W: What do you think of my idea?
   M: I can't come up with a better one, Mary.
   Q: What does the man think?

3. M: I'm so tired I think I'll go home now.
   W: I have to stay up until I finish the work.
   Q: What will the woman do?

4. W: Do you think we should park the car downtown?
   M: I don't know where we can.
   Q: What is being discussed?

5. W: Will you be joining us later?
   M: I need to catch up on the work I missed.
   Q: What can be said about the man?

6. M: I dozed off for most of the lecture.
   W: It almost put me to sleep, too.
   Q: What happened to the woman?

7. W: Which color would you choose?
   M: It makes no difference to me.
   Q: What do we learn from this talk?

8. M: Not everyone has as a good friend as Tom.
   W: I wish all of your friends were as nice.
   Q: What do we learn from this talk?

9. M: I read in the paper that the novel you're reading is excellent.
   W: I've also read some negative reviews.
   Q: What can be learned from this talk?

10. M: What have you been doing during your holiday?
    W: I haven't rested a bit. I've been jogging, weight-lifting and trying to get back into shape.
    Q: What has the woman been doing?

III. Directions: *In this section you will hear a passage of about 90 words three times. There are about 20 words missing. First, you will hear the whole passage from the beginning to the end just to get a general idea about it. Then, in the second reading, write down the missing words during the pauses. You can check what you have written when the passage is read to you once again without the pauses.*

Despite all the efforts that have been made, it remains **unknown** how these creatures find their way home. Since many of the birds **fly over** great bodies of water, we can't explain it **by saying** that they have **a sense of direction**. It is no good saying that they have **an instinct** to go home. These are just words, and **explain** nothing. The reason why they do it may be **to gain food** or to breed under the right conditions. But the **signals** they use on their flights are still **a mystery** to man.

Online Resources:

1. http://www.abc.net.au/rn/talks/8.30/sportsf/stories/s355733.htm
2. http://news.nationalgeographic.com/news/2003/11/1111_031111_earthquakeanimals.html
3. http://animals.about.com/b/a/047378.htm
4. http://www.cosic.esat.kuleuven.ac.be/nessie/
5. http://edu.sina.com.cn/en/2004-10-18/26650.html

Text Translation for Reference

第一单元 鲜为人知的事物

A 课文

信鸽如何找到自己的巢？

大家知道，一只一磅重的信鸽有着比最新式的喷气式飞机更好的引航设备，就这一点说，信鸽是很聪明的鸟儿。一只被带到陌生地方的信鸽，即使离鸟笼有几百英里之遥，几乎也能找到归巢的路。那信鸽又是如何找到的呢？这正是科学家急于想了解的事情。

这里有一些线索。实验表明鸽子不需要记住回程的路线。鸽子在熟睡时被蒙上眼睛带到离鸽巢很远的地方，并被置于转椅上，以混淆其方向感。然而当鸽子放飞时，几乎所有的信鸽仅需作一些尝试性的急转，就径直飞向自己的巢。即使鸽子的眼睛被蒙上模糊不清的"隐形眼镜"，它们也能返回自己的家。这证明鸽子并不只是依赖眼力来决定其飞行计划的。

那么鸽子又是怎么做到的呢？也许是因为磁力的原因吧。整个地球被磁场覆盖着，北极吸引磁性物质，就像吸引指南针的指针一样；而南极排斥磁性物质。研究人员已经发现在鸽子的颈部肌肉中存在着微小的磁性物质，鸽子可能感到在其颈部有一种朝北的引力，并与它在笼子里所感到的磁力作比较。这种不同的引力能使鸽子辨别不同的方向。

然而,看起来很明显,远远不只是磁力在起作用。研究人员在一些信鸽颈部系上小块的磁铁棒,然后将它们放飞。磁铁棒具有强大的磁场,足以阻止地球的磁性引力。如果信鸽仅仅是依靠地球的磁场来确定方向,那么它们的飞行就会混乱不堪。

某些鸽子确实发生过这样的事情。如果是阴天,飞行的鸽子就会迷路;如果天晴,它们就能找到归巢的路。因此这很有可能说明鸽子是靠太阳和磁场来引航的。

这其中仍然存在着更多的可能性。意大利的研究人员将一些鸽子的鼻孔堵住,然后放飞,它们返回就会有一定困难,这表明嗅觉因素也包含其中。其他测试显示鸽子在地球引力中能觉察微小的变化,它们能比人类察觉范围更广的光亮和声音。这些可能性中的任意一项或所有项目都能帮助鸽子返回自己的巢。

鸽子到底是怎样运用所有这些感觉的还是个谜。它们天生就能辨认地球的磁场图吗?它们能算出太阳的角度吗?它们又是怎样利用所接收到的视觉、嗅觉和声音来制定其飞行图呢?最后,它们将所有的信息保存在小小鸽脑的哪个部位呢?

这个谜团还远远没有解开。

B 课文

动物是怎样预知地震来临的?

近来,那些试图预测地震的科学家们从动物身上获得了一些新的启发。

确实如此,动物能够帮助科学家预测地震。科学家们已经开始理解几千年来农民所掌握的相关知识。当地震来临时,动物是怎样知道的?虽然有些人认为对这个问题的研究毫无用处,但是科学家们仍在努力地进行研究。

动物似乎能预知地震的来临,而且它们通过各种奇特的方式来表现出自己的恐惧。1975年,在中国的一次地震爆发前,蛇很早就从冬眠中苏醒过来,不料却冻死在寒风里;奶牛挣断缰绳,试图逃跑;鸡群也拒绝进入鸡笼。所有这些反常的举动,加上地球上的一些物理变化,都警告着中国科学家一场地震将要来临。他们告知人们迁出危险的地区,从而拯救了成千上万的生命。

科学家有必要准确地知道动物习性的哪些类型能预报地震。当然这不是一项简单的工作。首先,并非每一种动物都能对地震的危险做出反应。就是在 1977 年加利福尼亚地震前,一匹阿拉伯马变得非常焦躁不安,想冲出马厩,但是与此相邻的马匹却相当的安闲。有时人们也很难分辨正常情况下焦躁不安的动物和患有"地震神经质"的动物之间的差别。一位动物园的饲养员曾告诉地震研究人员,园里的美洲豹行为异常,后来发现原来是美洲豹的胃有问题。

对科学家来说,准确地查明动物感觉到的预警到底是哪些类型同样是非常必要的。他们知道,动物能比人类感觉到世界上更多的现象。很多动物能看见人类根本觉察不到的东西,能听见人类听不到的声音,并能闻到一些人类闻不到的气味,有些动物还能察觉到在地心引力或地球磁场中的微小变化,有可能正是这种感觉使得动物能预测地震。

发生在一群狗身上的故事就是很好的例子。它们被关在一个正发生一系列微震的地区。众所周知,在强震到来的前后,常常会伴有微震。每一次地震前总会听到低沉的隆隆声,每一阵隆隆声都会导致一阵疯狂的犬吠。当时,这群狗竟然在安静的时段里开始狂叫。一位观察记录地震的科学家观看了仪器,这仪器似乎也测出有很大的噪音。科学家意识到狗群已对隆隆的噪声做出反应,它们也感觉到了随之而来的微震。虽然人类没有察觉到任何情况,也没听到任何动静,但仪器却都有记录。

  在这个事例中,仪器可以用来监测狗察觉到的一切情况。然而在很多情况下,尽管动物知道了地震的来临,可是仪器却无法记录下任何异常的情况。一些我们尚不知道如何测定的事情,或者一些我们确实测定过,但并没有意识到是前兆的事情,动物却有可能感觉到了。发现动物察觉到了什么,搞清动物怎样辨认出危险信号,这是未来科学家的任务。

Unit Two

FIGHT AGAINST AIDS

Objective

By the end of this unit, the learners are required to grasp the following:

I. Key Words and Phrases

1. Words:

   lead, leader, leading
   respire, respiration, respiratory
   isolate, isolated, isolating, isolation
   suffice, sufficiency, sufficient, insufficient
   pervious, previously

2. Phrases:

   at the outset   be associated with   be accompanied by   behave oneself
   die of   in an attempt to   in the meantime   on board
   respond to   settle into

II. Language Structure

Direct Speech and Indirect Speech

III. Practice and Improvement

Reading Skills: Speed Reading and Cloze Procedure
Speaking Skills: Seeing the Doctor
Listening Skills: Sound Recognition, Dialogues, and Spot Dictation
Translation Skills: Phrases and Direct Speech and Indirect Speech
Writing Skills: Sentence Patterns and Letters

Word Usage

Reading Selection

Text A

1) Nelson Mandela **made an impassioned plea** on Friday, July 16th, 2004 at the 15th International AIDS conference for cash and cooperation to fight the killer AIDS virus after a week of discord at the world's biggest AIDS conference held in Bangkok, Thailand.

   make a plea　主张，请求

   e.g.　He made a plea for help.
   他请求帮助。

2) "History will surely judge us harshly if we do not **respond** with all the energy and resources that we can bring to bear in the **fight against** AIDS," said the former South African President, who would turn 86 on the following day.

   respond　*v.*　to say or do something as a reaction to something that has been said or done
   回答，响应，做出反应

   response　*n.*　an answer or reaction　回答，回应，反应

   responsible　*adj.*　(常与 to, for 连用)有责任的，应负责任的

   responsibility　*n.*　something that it is your job or duty to deal with　责任，职责，义务，常与 for, of, to 连用

   e.g.　The plane responds well to the controls.
   这架飞机对操纵反应灵敏。

   He responded that he wouldn't go.
   他回答说他不去。

   She got little response from the audience.
   听众对她几乎没什么反应。

   I'm getting a strong response on the sonar.
   我在声纳上测得强力反应。

   The bus driver is responsible for the passengers' safety.
   公共汽车司机应对乘客的安全负责。

   The police are responsible for the preservation of public order and security.
   警察有责任维护公共秩序和安全。

   I am responsible for my sister until she gets a job.
   在我妹妹找到工作以前，我对她负责。

I will take the responsibility of (for) doing it.
我会负责做那件事。
I did it on my own responsibility.
我自作主张地做了这件事。

3) **Wrapping up** the week-long 15th International AIDS conference, Mr. Mandela urged the world's rich countries to keep their financial promises to the Global Fund to combat AIDS launched in 2002.

wrap　*v.*　to cover or enclose something with paper, cloth or other material　裹，包；覆盖

wrap up
① to dress in warm clothes, or to dress someone in warm clothes　多穿衣服，穿得暖和
② to cover or enclose something in paper, cloth or other material　包起来，裹起来
③ to complete something successfully　[口]完成，结束

e.g.　*He wrapped the book in a piece of paper.*
他用纸把那本书包了起来。
The affair is wrapped in mystery.
这件事真相不明。
He wrapped himself up in a coat, because it's cold outside.
外面冷着呢，他把身子裹在外衣里。
Have you wrapped up Jenny's present yet?
你把詹妮的礼物包好了吗？
Let's wrap up the job and go home.
我们做完工作就回家吧。
Now the agreement is wrapped up, all we have to do is to wait for the first orders.
现在协议签订完了，我们要做的事便是等第一批订单。

4) "We need to build the public-private partnership that is the vision of the Global Fund. We challenge everyone to help fund the fund now," **called on** Mr. Mandela...

call on　号召，呼吁；访问

e.g.　*The president called on the citizens to work hard for national unity.*
总统号召公民们为了国家的统一而努力工作。
An old friend called on me the day before yesterday.
前天一位老朋友来找过我。
The retired director called on at your office yesterday.
已经退休了的董事昨天到你办公室来看过你。
We can call on our former teacher tomorrow.
我们明天可以去拜访过去的老师。

5) "If we did not collect enough fund and cooperate effectively, we might fail to **halt** AIDS next year," Kofi Annan warned the delegates.

 halt *n.* when something stops moving or happening 停止,暂停,中断

    v. to (cause to) stop moving or doing something 使停止,使立定

 e.g. The car comes to a halt.
    汽车停了下来。
    The officer called a halt.
    军官下令停止前进。
    No one can halt the advance of history.
    谁也阻挡不了历史的前进。
    They halted the operation on account of the bad weather.
    由于天气不好他们暂时停止军事演习。
    The soldiers halted for a short rest.
    士兵们停下来休息一会儿。

6) He also required the general public to **eliminate** any forms of **discrimination** against AIDS victims.

 eliminate *v.* to remove or take away 排除,消除,除去

 e.g. She has been eliminated from the swimming race because she did not win any of the practice races.
    她已被取消了游泳比赛资格,因为她在训练中没有得到名次。
    We should eliminate sex barriers.
    我们应该消除男女的差别。
    Please eliminate the unnecessary words from the essay.
    请把不必要的字从论文中删去。

 discriminate *v.* to treat differently 歧视,区别,区别待遇

 discrimination *n.* 辨别,区别;识别力,辨别力;歧视

 discriminatory *adj.* 有辨识力的;有差别的;歧视的

 e.g. This new law discriminates against lower-paid colored workers.
    这项新法律歧视低工资的有色人种的工人。
    When you come to a composition, you must try to discriminate between facts and opinions.
    写作文时你要设法把事实和看法区别开来。
    Can you discriminate good books from bad?
    你能区别好书和坏书吗?
    He has a fine discrimination in choosing wine.
    他有品酒的鉴别力。
    Discrimination against women is not allowed.
    歧视妇女是不能允许的。

Racism or discriminatory conduct has no place in the small town.
这座小城没有种族主义或歧视行为。

7) However, Washington **ruled out** raising its contribution to the fund beyond USD200 million already committed for next year...

rule out 排除,划去

e.g.   But this does not rule out unofficial discussions.
但这并不排除进行非正式的讨论。
We can't rule out the possibility that he'll change his mind.
我们不能排除他改变主意的可能性。
The regulations rule out anyone under the age of 18.
规则规定18岁以下的人都不能参加。

8) The conference activists hoped that the conference had served as a rallying point against AIDS, especially in Asia, home to 60 percent of humanity and a quarter of all new **infections**.

infect   *v.*   to pass a disease to a person, animal or plant   传染,感染
infection   *n.*   传染,感染
infectious   *adj.*   有传染性的,易传染的;有感染力的
infectiously   *adv.*

e.g.   One of the boys in the class had a fever and he soon infected other children.
班上的一个孩子发烧了,不久他就传染上了其他孩子。
If your eyes are infected, you must go to an oculist.
如果你的眼睛受到感染,就要去看眼科医生。
She infected the whole class with her laughter.
她的笑声感染了全班同学。
Mary's high spirits infected all the girls in the class.
玛丽振奋的精神感染了班上所有的女孩子。
Colds are infectious, and so are some eye diseases.
感冒是传染的,有些眼病也是传染的。
She raised an infectious laugh.
她发出了有感染力的笑声。

9) India, where 5.1 million people **suffered from** AIDS—the world's second highest after South Africa—was finally getting the clear message after years of **criticism** over foot-dragging and denial, said ruling Congress Party leader Sonia Gandhi.

suffer from   to experience or show the effects of something bad   忍受,遭受;患病

e.g.   These areas suffered greatly from floods.
这个地区遭受了严重的水灾。

The child suffers from measles.
这个小孩得了麻疹。

critic *n.* someone who says that they do not approve of someone or something 批评家, 评论家;吹毛求疵者

critical *adj.* 评论的,鉴定的;批评的;危急的;临界的

criticize *v.* to express disapproval of someone or something 批评;吹毛求疵;非难

e.g. *It is a book drubbed by every critic.*
这是一本受到所有批评家抨击的书。

He is a sports critic.
他是一位体育评论家。

He put forward his critical opinions on this latest play.
他提出了自己有关这出新剧的评论意见。

He is a man with a critical eye.
他是一个具有批判眼光的人。

He always picks on small points to criticize.
他老是找些小问题进行批评。

The government is being widely criticized in the press for failing to limit air pollution.
政府因为没能减少空气污染而受到媒体广泛的批评。

10) "Today, let us **renew our commitment** to work together to reach out our hands with compassion to the millions of men, women and children who are the tragic victims of the physical and social devastation caused by HIV," Mrs. Gandhi **appealed to** the delegates finally.

commitment *n.* 许诺,承担义务

renew one's commitment 重新承担责任(义务)

e.g. *I've taken on too many commitments.*
我承担的义务太多了。

He doesn't want to get married because he is afraid of any commitments.
他不想结婚,因为他害怕承担任何责任。

Various governments in the world have decided to renew their commitments to combat AIDS with all the energy and resources.
世界上很多国家已决定重新承担其责任,竭尽全力抗击艾滋病。

appeal to 呼吁,要求,诉诸,上诉;有吸引力

e.g. *Farmers have appealed to the government for help.*
农民已经呼吁政府给予帮助。

The police appealed to the crowd not to panic.
警察要求人群不要惊慌。

She appealed to the high court against her sentence.
她不服判决而向高等法院上诉。

Bright colors appeal to small children.
小孩喜欢鲜艳的颜色。
The idea of working abroad really appeals to me.
去国外工作的想法的确让我感兴趣。

Outline:

1. Nelson Mandela made an impassioned plea to fight the killer AIDS virus at the 15th International AIDS Conference. (Para. 1-5)
2. Kofi Annan said that the Global Fund needed more than USD3 billion for 2005 to present a global, unified force against HIV and AIDS in 2005. (Para. 6-7)
3. The response of Washington to the fund. (Para. 8-9)
4. The practical situation of AIDS in Asia, especially in India. (Para. 10-11)
5. Mrs. Gandhi required the international society never to neglect the hopeless people caused by HIV. (Para. 12-13)
6. The timetable of the 15th International AIDS Conference. (Para. 14)

Text B

1) New York Conference **Focuses on** AIDS Vaccine Development
   focus on   集中
   e.g. *All eyes were focused on him.*
   大家把目光都集中在他身上。
   Public attention at the moment is focused on the problem of pollution.
   目前,公众的注意力都集中在污染问题上。

2) At the AIDS Vaccine Conference in New York, on Thursday, September 17, 2003, there was a **call for** faster and broader testing of experimental vaccines.
   call for   要求,提倡,为……叫喊
   e.g. *Our class calls for a debate on the subject.*
   我们班级要求对这个问题进行辩论。
   The occasion calls for a cool head.
   这种场合需要冷静的头脑。
   Someone is calling for help.
   有人在大声呼救。

3) With an estimated 44-million people suffering from HIV/AIDS, **medical** researchers said only a vaccine could halt the high rate of infection.
   medicine   *n.*   treatment for illness or injury, or the study of this   药;医学,医术
   medical   *adj.*   related to the treatment of illness and injuries   医学的,内科的

medically   *adv.*   医学上，医药上

e.g.   *This is a good medicine for colds.*
这是一种治疗感冒的良药。
Anesthesia was a great innovation in medicine.
麻醉是一项伟大的医学创新。
My parents hoped I would study medicine, but I didn't want to.
我父母亲希望我学医，但是我不愿意。
The demand for medical men is urgent right now.
当前迫切需要医务人员。
This hospital has 20 medical wards.
这所医院有20个内科病房。

4) Obviously, we're still far from the development of a completely **protective** and practical vaccine.

protect   *v.*   to keep someone or something safe from injury, damage or loss   保护（常与 from, against 连用）

protection   *n.*   the act of protecting or state of being protected   保护，警戒（from, against）

protective   *adj.*   giving protection   保护(性)的，防护的，预防的

e.g.   *A line of forts was built along the border to protect the country against attack.*
在边界沿线构筑了堡垒，以防国家受到攻击。
He raised his arm to protect his face.
他举起手臂护住脸部。
The protection of the country is the duty of everyone.
保卫国家是每个人的责任。
Her coat gave her protection from the rain.
她的外套使她免受雨淋之苦。
She's too protective towards her son.
她过于呵护儿子。

5) But Dr. Karim said there was some encouraging news. He said, "AIDS vaccine testing has taken on a much more global hue..."

take on   披上；呈现；具有；雇用；承担

e.g.   *Diana always takes on too much work.*
黛安娜总是承担太多的工作。
The ship will stop at Shanghai to take on passengers and mail.
这艘船将在上海停泊，去接乘客和邮件。
He was taken on by a factory as a worker.
他被一家工厂录用当工人。

After the students put up Christmas decorations, the classroom took on a holiday appearance.
学生们布置好圣诞饰物时,教室里便呈现出节日的景象。

6) He said, "There are three basic reasons why it has been difficult to **come up with** a successful AIDS vaccine especially one that will work in developing countries."
   come up with   赶上;提出
   e.g. *We are making our efforts to come up with advanced level.*
   我们正在努力赶上先进水平。
   He first came up with the good idea of going to visit a factory.
   是他首先提出去参观工厂这个好主意的。
   He couldn't come up with an answer.
   他答不上来。
   He couldn't come up with an appropriate answer just at the time.
   那时他想不出一个合适的答案。

7) The conference **ran through** Sunday, September 21, 2003.
   run through   贯穿;匆匆处理;划掉;跑着穿过;挥霍;排练
   e.g. *Let's run through this song once again.*
   咱们再唱一遍这首歌。
   Don't run through your work so fast.
   做这工作不要这么赶。
   The heir soon ran through his fortune.
   那个继承人很快就把资财耗尽了。
   I'll just run through this list of figures.
   我将把这个数字表检查一遍。
   Could you run through the procedure, please?
   你能大概演示一下生产过程吗?

Summary:

   At the AIDS Vaccine Conference in New York, there was a call for faster and broader testing of experimental vaccines to halt the high rate of infection. Even though many countries were developing their own vaccines, we were still far from the development of a completely protective and practical vaccine. There are three basic reasons why it had been difficult to come up with a successful AIDS vaccine.

Key to Unit 2

Exercises for Reading Comprehension

I. Answer the following questions.

1. Mr. Mandela made an impassioned plea on Friday July 16th, 2004 at the 15th International AIDS conference in Bangkok, Thailand.
2. He made the impassioned plea for cash and cooperation to fight the killer, AIDS virus.
3. History will surely judge us harshly if we do not respond with all the energy and resources that we can bring to bear in the fight against AIDS.
4. It lasted a whole week.
5. Mr. Mandela urged the world's rich countries to keep their financial promises to the Global Fund to fight AIDS, malaria and tuberculosis launched in 2002.
6. The Global Fund needs more than US$3 billion for 2005 to present a global, unified force against HIV and AIDS, according to Kofi Annan.
7. The United States was criticized by all sides, including Nelson Mandela and Kofi Annan.
8. The conference activists hoped that the conference had served as a rallying point against AIDS, especially in Asia.
9. 5.1 million people suffer from AIDS in India.
10. "Today, let us renew our commitment to work together to reach out our hands with compassion to the millions of men, women and children who are the tragic victims of the physical and social devastation caused by HIV," Mrs. Gandhi appealed to the delegates finally.
11. The AIDS Vaccine Conference was held in New York, on Thursday, September 17, 2003.
12. More than 1,200 people from 50 countries gathered for the meeting.
13. Researchers said only a vaccine could halt the high rate of infection.
14. No, they haven't. They're still far from the development of a completely protective and practical vaccine.
15. He is a leading vaccine researcher at the University of Natal in South Africa.
16. Because there was no vaccine.
17. Yes, there was.
18. 24,000 of his fellow countrymen in South Africa would become infected with HIV.
19. Vaccine testing has taken on a much more global hue, for example, trials are underway in Trinidad, Brazil, Uganda and Thailand. And more countries, such as China and India, are developing their own vaccines.
20. Yes, I can. The first is that the epidemiology of HIV is dramatically different in these settings. The second problem is there are many different sub-types of HIV and they can vary from region to region; and finally, people's genetic makeup may determine whether a particular vaccine works for them.

II. **Find the meanings of the words or expressions in Column (A) from those in Column (B).**
   1. A   2. G   3. I   4. B   5. E   6. F   7. C   8. D   9. H   10. J

III. **Complete the sentences with the given expressions, and change the forms where necessary.**
   1. called on... to reach out
   2. are infected with
   3. fight against
   4. has ruled out... suffered from
   5. are focusing on
   6. came up with
   7. to renew their commitment
   8. has taken on
   9. am appealing to
   10. running through

IV. **Fill in the blanks with the words listed below, and be sure to use appropriate verb forms and appropriate singular and plural forms for nouns.**
   1. infectious, infected, infection
   2. discriminate, discriminatory, discrimination
   3. criticized, critics, criticism, critical
   4. protect, protective, protection
   5. respond, response, responsible, responsibility

V. **Complete the following passage by using appropriate words listed below, and be sure to use singular or plural forms for nouns.**
   1. eliminate   2. treatment   3. medical   4. urgency   5. mobilize
   6. encouraging   7. campaign   8. halt   9. responsibility   10. fatal

Exercises for Language Structure

I. **Rewrite the following sentences after the model, changing the direct speech into the indirect speech or changing the indirect speech into the direct speech.**
   1. Li Ping said that he thought that those symptoms of AIDS were very terrible.
   2. Ann said, "I have had a lot of friends in my junior school days."
   3. A delegate from South Africa said that the conference was about mobilizing Asia not to go down the route that Africa had gone.
   4. Mr. Mandela asked the 19, 843 delegates to allow him to enjoy his retirement by showing they could rise to the challenge.
   5. Sue asked her new friend what she/he was planning to do during that special period of preventing SARS.
   6. Mother asked Sandra, "Have you finished the report about the cause of AIDS?"
   7. Paul asked Stephanie if she was going to take part in the English speech competition.
   8. Li Hao asked Lin Tao, "Have you ever been to the World Window Park?"
   9. Mother asked her daughter how she was getting on with her new classmates.
   10. Sue asked Bob, "Will AIDS become a global pandemic or settle into a less aggressive pattern?"

II. Fill in the blanks with the sentences listed below, and be sure to change the direct speech into the indirect speech.

1. Bill was taking a long time to get ready, so I told him to hurry up.
2. Sarah was driving too fast, so I asked her to slow down.
3. Sue was ill in hospital, so I told her not to worry.
4. I couldn't move the piano alone, so I asked Tom to give me a hand.
5. The customs officer looked at me suspiciously and told me to open my bag.
6. I had difficulty understanding him, so I asked him to repeat.
7. I'm going away for a holiday, so I asked Mary to take care of my dog.
8. I didn't want to delay Ann, so I told her not to wait for me if I was late.
9. John was very much in love with Mary, so he asked her to marry him.
10. He started asking me personal questions, so I told him to mind his own business.

III. Choose the best answer.

1. A   2. A   3. D   4. D   5. D   6. B   7. A   8. B   9. A   10. C

IV. Find out which of the underlined parts in each sentence is not correct in written English.

1. D. ago 改为 before
2. A. said to me 改为 told me
3. B. doesn't 改为 not to
4. B. is 改为 was
5. B. if 改为 that if
6. B. has 改为 had
7. D. this 改为 that
8. D. him and she 改为 him and her
9. B. have thought 改为 had thought
10. C. are 改为 were

Practice and Improvement

Reading Skills

Speed Reading I
1. B   2. C   3. D   4. D   5. A   6. F   7. T   8. T   9. F   10. F

Speed Reading II
1. A   2. C   3. D   4. D   5. C   6. T   7. F   8. F   9. F   10. T

Cloze Procedure
1. A   2. B   3. A   4. C   5. D   6. A   7. B   8. C   9. D   10. C

Communication Function

II. Conversation

Seeing a Doctor

A: Good afternoon! How can I help you today?

B: Doctor, I have a terrible cold. Is there anything you can do to help me?

A: Let me take your temperature first. (Checks eyes, ears, pulse, etc.) Well, you have a slight fever. It seems at this point to be nothing serious, but you need to get plenty of rest and drink a lot of water. Also, eat healthy food, and take this medicine.

B: But, doctor, I don't have time to rest. Our factory is having an inspection next week, and I'm in charge of getting everything in order.

A: I understand your problem. However, if you don't get plenty of rest, your cold could get worse and you might end up in hospital next week. You must take care of your health first.

B: Okay. Thank you very much. It's very kind of you.

A: You're welcome. See you.

B: See you!

Listening Comprehension

I. 1. B 2. A 3. B 4. A 5. A 6. B 7. A 8. B 9. B 10. A

II. 1. A 2. B 3. B 4. C 5. B 6. B 7. D 8. D 9. C 10. A

III.
1. December first
2. at events
3. Let Live
4. with HIV and AIDS
5. prevention and treatment
6. shows no signs
7. 40 million
8. 2.5 million
9. become infected with
10. in 2004

Translation Skills

I. Translate the following into English.

1. Wrapping up the week-long 15th International AIDS conference, Mr. Mandela urged the world's rich countries to keep their financial promises to the Global Fund to fight AIDS.
2. AIDS has already claimed (killed) 20 million lives and infected twice as much worldwide.
3. Kofi Annan, the United Nations Secretary-General, required the general public to eliminate any forms of discrimination against AIDS victims.
4. Sexual contact, infected blood and the sharing of injection needles can all spread the AIDS virus.

5. As AIDS continues to stretch quickly around the globe, parents want to know what they can do to prevent their kids from getting it.

II. Translate the following into Chinese.
1. 曼德拉先生对19840名与会代表说:"请你们奋起面对挑战,让我享受退休生活吧。"
2. 卡利姆博士说:"艾滋疫苗的实验已经具有更加全球化的色彩。"
3. 甘地夫人说她曾经遇到过一些被社区排除在外的艾滋病受害者。
4. 曼德拉先生敦促世界富裕国家信守其对2002年发起成立的防治艾滋病全球基金提供财政支持的承诺。
5. 她呼吁与会代表向无助的艾滋病受害者伸出援助之手。

Writing Skills

I. Rewrite each of the sentences after the models.

Model A:
1. Mrs. Gandhi required the delegates to renew their commitments to reach out their hands to the tragic AIDS patients.
2. Kofi Annan called on the international society to give timely aid to the victims caused by the Indian Ocean Tsunami.
3. Wang Hong asked the audience to allow her to extend their heartfelt thanks to the teachers who had given the students so much help.
4. The boss told the clerk to go to his office at 8 o'clock the next day.
5. Prof. Bradley ordered the students to hand in their exercise-books that afternoon.

Model B:
1. The nurse said to the patients, "Don't share the injection needles with others."
2. "Don't waste the raw materials," he said to the workers.
3. "Don't withdraw from the defense work," the general ordered his soldiers.
4. "Never do your assignments carelessly," Prof. Bradley said to the students.
5. "Never look down upon the market function," the economist said to the government officials.

II. Practical Writing

A Letter

                                                   26 Jingkui Road Changsha   信头

                                                 Hunan, 410004

                                                 P.R.China

Dr. Barton Haynes   信内地址
Medical Center, Duke University
Durham, NC23562
United States

                                                April 14, 2005   日期

Dear Prof. Haynes,   称呼

    Please excuse me for taking some of your time with this unexpected   正文
letter. I'm a student in the Biological Department of Changsha Polytechnic of Environmental Protection. I have read one of your theses on Prevention of AIDS in the *Health* magazine and I'm glad that you will pay a visit to China next week.

    Recently, people in some places suffer from AIDS terribly, so our college has launched a campaign to prevent AIDS.

    I'm the chairman of the Students' Union. Next week, we plan to have a lecture on the prevention of AIDS, and we'd like to invite you to give us a report on how to prevent AIDS. If you are free at that time, we'll give you a warm welcome.

    I'm looking forward to your early reply.

                                                          Yours Sincerely,   结束语
                                                              Dong Mei   签名

Tape Scripts for Listening Comprehension

I. Directions: *Listen to the following sentences. Choose which word the speaker or the tape says. Tick the right word.*

1. We challenge everyone to help **fund** the fund now.
2. Some people who suffer from AIDS can no longer hope to raise and **bear** healthy children.
3. Allow me to enjoy my retirement by showing you can **rise** to the challenge.
4. We **need** to build the public-private partnership that is the vision of the Global Fund.

5. If you take Southern Africa, most of the people becoming **infected** are young and they are women.
6. More than 1,200 people from **50** countries gathered for the New York Conference.
7. The Global Fund needs more than USD3 **billion** for 2005 to present a global, unified force against HIV and AIDS.
8. "If we did not collect enough money, we might fail to halt AIDS next year," Kofi Annan **warned** the delegates.
9. The test can tell if they have been threatened by **blood** from infected patients.
10. Currently, about half the people tested for HIV in public health centers fail to return to learn the results of the **test**.

II. **Directions:** *In this section, you will hear 10 short conversations. At the end of each conversation, a question will be asked about what was said. The conversation and the question will be spoken only one time. After each question, there will be a pause. During the pause, you must read the four choices marked A, B, C and D, and decide which the best answer is, and then choose the corresponding letter.*

1. W: Let's go to the fast restaurant before the movies.
   M: I'd rather eat afterwards.
   Q: What does the woman want to do?

2. W: Make sure you bring a bathing suit.
   M: And you bring the towel and a picnic lunch.
   Q: Where are they going?

3. M: Have you seen Kathy's new red car?
   W: She was lucky. She got it on sale from the dealer before he closed down.
   Q: What happened to the car dealer?

4. W: Keep your eye out for a one-bedroom apartment for me.
   M: I hear there are several vacancies in the new hotel downtown.
   Q: What does the woman want the man to do?

5. M: Even though you are not crazy about my friends, let's have a party next Saturday.
   W: Ok, but you take care of all the arrangements.
   Q: What does the man want?

6. M: Where did Mary get that new skirt?
   W: She had a tailor remake an old one.
   Q: Where did Mary get the skirt?

7. W: You should have finished the book before it was due.
   M: I know. Now I'll have to pay a huge sum of money.
   Q: What will the man have to do?

8. M: Mary made up for the time she missed by working overtime.
   W: That's why I saw her working the weekend shift.
   Q: What did Mary do?

9. M: Registration always takes so long.
   W: What bothers me is all the people who cut in line.
   Q: What bothers the woman?
10. W: Should we get Tim a record for his birthday?
    M: Just because he's a composer doesn't mean he only likes listening to music.
    Q: What did the man say?

III. Directions: *In this section you will hear a passage of about 90 words three times. There are about 20 words missing. First, you will hear the whole passage from the beginning to the end just to get a general idea about it. Then, in the second reading, write down the missing words during the pauses. You can check what you have written when the passage is read to you once again without the pauses.*

  December first is World AIDS Day. The message **at events** this year is "Live and **Let Live.**" The aim is to end improper treatment of people **with HIV and AIDS**. Experts say such discrimination remains a barrier to **prevention and treatment**. The United Nations reported last week that the spread of AIDS **shows no signs** of easing. It says an estimated **40 million** people are living with the HIV virus. These include **2.5 million** children. Worldwide, the report said that 6 million people **became infected with** HIV and 5 million died **in 2004**—the most ever.

Online Resources:
1. http://au.news.yahoo.com/050825/19/vnsn.html
2. http://www.unaids.org/en/default.asp
3. http://fightaidsathome.scripps.edu/
4. http://www.aids.org/
5. http://www.avert.org/worldaid.htm

Text Translation for Reference

第二单元　与艾滋病作斗争

A 课文

防治艾滋病的斗争需要更多的资金和合作

  世界规模最大的防治艾滋病会议在泰国曼谷召开。经过历时一周的嘈杂争论之后，纳尔逊·曼德拉于2004年7月14日星期五，在第15届国际防治艾滋病会议上热情洋溢地呼吁全球各国要为战胜艾滋病毒杀手投入资金并进行合作。

"在防治艾滋病的斗争中,如果我们不能动用我们的全部精力和资源进行应对,历史肯定会对我们做出严厉的评判。"南非前总统说了上述这番话,次日他将步入86岁高龄。

在结束为期一周的第15届国际防治艾滋病会议时,曼德拉先生敦促世界富裕国家信守其对2002年发起成立的防治艾滋病全球基金提供财政支持的承诺。

"我们需要建立公私合作关系,这就是具有先见之明的防治艾滋病全球基金。我们要求每个人都帮助募集资金。"曼德拉先生号召说。曼德拉先生是诺贝尔和平奖得主,也是世界上主要的防治艾滋病的宣传活动家之一。

曼德拉先生对与会的19843名代表说,"请你们奋起迎接挑战,让我安享退休生活吧。"

据联合国秘书长科菲·安南说,2005年全球基金需要30多亿美元来部署一个全球统一的力量来防治艾滋病。

科菲·安南告诫与会代表:"如果我们不能筹措到足够的资金并进行有效的合作,我们也许无法在明年遏制艾滋病的蔓延。"他还要求公众消除对艾滋病受害者的任何歧视。

然而,华盛顿(美国政府)否认了在已承担明年费用两亿美元的基础上增加对全球基金的捐款,并说美国在防治这一致命疾病方面的花费比世界其他地区合在一起的花费还多。

尽管美国遭到了包括纳尔逊·曼德拉和科菲·安南在内的与会各方对其道义责任和基金方针的批评,美国全球防治艾滋病协调人兰德尔·托拜厄斯仍坚持认为美国正在领导防治艾滋病的斗争。艾滋病已经夺去了两千万人的生命,而被感染的人数多达死者的两倍。

与会的活动家希望这次大会已经起到了汇聚力量防治艾滋病的作用,尤其对亚洲来说。亚洲是地球上60%人类的家园,但艾滋病的新患者却占了四分之一。一位南非代表说:"这次会议将动员亚洲不要重蹈南非的覆辙。"

印度执政的国大党领导人索尼亚·甘地说,印度在行动迟缓失误遭到多年批评之后终于获得了明确的信息。印度有510万艾滋病患者,患者人数之多高居世界第二位,仅次于南非。

甘地夫人在会议闭幕式上说:"我曾会见过那些失去工作的人,那些被社区排斥的人,那些不再抱有希望抚养健康孩子的人。"她要求国际社会千万不要疏忽那些无助的人们。

甘地夫人最后向与会代表呼吁说:"今天让我们重新承担我们的责任,共同工作,满怀怜悯之心向数百万由于艾滋病毒而饱受身心和社会之害的男女和儿童伸出援助之手。"

B 课文

纽约会议集中探讨艾滋病疫苗的研发

2003年9月17日星期四在纽约召开的艾滋病疫苗会议号召加快进行范围更广的实验性疫苗的测试工作。来自50个国家的1200多人汇聚纽约,参加了这次大会。

由于约4400万人患有艾滋病,医学研究人员说只有疫苗才能抑制这种高传染率疾病。然而,研发成功的疫苗仍然需要几年的时间。

杜克大学的巴顿·海恩斯博士是大会的组织者之一。他说:"尽管在过去的几年里已经完成了不少的科学研究,但需要做的事情会更多。显然,我们还远未研发出能起完全保护作用的实用性疫苗。"

南非纳塔尔大学艾滋病疫苗研究带头人萨利姆·卡利姆说:"没有疫苗,这种流行病每天都会进一步蔓延。仅在我与会的三天时间里,我在南非的24000个同胞就会染上艾滋病毒。"

但是卡利姆博士说也有一些令人鼓舞的消息。他说:"艾滋病疫苗的实验工作已经更具全球化的色彩。例如,在特立尼达、巴西、乌干达和泰国,疫苗试验正在进行之中。更多的国家,如中国和印度,正在研发自己的疫苗。"

他说:"难以提供成功的艾滋病疫苗——尤其在发展中国家能见效的艾滋病疫苗的基本原因有三个。什么是成功的艾滋病疫苗,谁将使用这种疫苗,何时何地使用这种疫苗,为什么要使用这种疫苗,怎样使用这种疫苗真是一个令人困惑的问题,否则这种广为传染的疾病就不会被称为流行病了。"

"首先,艾滋流行病毒在各种环境下具有明显的差别。如在南部非洲,感染艾滋病的大部分人是青年妇女。以我国南非为例,妇女感染的人数为男子的两倍。"

"第二个问题是存在许多不同的亚类型艾滋病毒,而且这些病毒随着地区间的差异而变化。"最后,他说:"人们的基因结构可以决定某种特殊的疫苗是否对他们有效。"

这次会议将持续到2003年9月21日,星期日。

Unit Three

ENERGY SENSE MAKES FUTURE SENSE

Objective

By the end of this unit, the learners are required to grasp the following:

I. Key Words and Phrases

1. Words:

| atomic | chemical | electric | heat | kinetic |
| light | mechanical | muscular | potential | radiant |

2. Phrases:

| begin with | boil away | burn out | give off | plunge... into |
| provide... for | push against | safe and sound | supply... with | turn away |

II. Language Structure

The Subjunctive Mood

III. Practice and Improvement

Reading Skills: Speed Reading and Cloze Procedure
Speaking Skills: Asking for Advice
Listening Skills: Sentence Judgment, Dialogues, and Spot Dictation
Translation Skills: Phrases and the Subjunctive Mood
Writing Skills: Sentence Patterns and Pacts & Rules

Word Usage

Reading Selection

Text A

1) If you think about some of the important **transformation** of energy, you will understand why this is true.

   transform   *v.*   to change completely the appearance or character of something or someone, especially so that they are improved   转变

   transformation   *n.*   改变

   transformer   *n.*   a device which changes the voltage or other characteristics of electrical energy as it moves from one circuit to another   变压器

   transformable   *adj.*   to be convertible into something   可转换的

   e.g.   The reorganization will transform the British entertainment industry.
   重组能改变英国的娱乐业。
   Local people have mixed feelings about the planned transformation of their town into a regional capital.
   那个地区的人们对于要把他们居住的城镇变成地辖市的计划有着一种复杂的情感。
   I'd never seen Carlo in smart evening clothes before—it was quite a transformation.
   我以前从没见过卡罗穿着时髦的晚礼服——这真是个大转变。

2) This energy **is** often **supplied** by some kind of engine that burns fuel.

   supply   *v.*   to provide something that is wanted or needed, often in large quantities and over a long period of time   提供

   supply... with sth   以某物供应

   supply... for sb   向某人供应

   supply   *n.*   an amount of something that is available for use   供应物

   supplier   *n.*   a company, person, etc. that provides things that people want or need, especially over a long period of time   供应商

   e.g.   The shop was unable to supply what she wanted.
   这商店不能提供她所需要的商品。
   At the beginning of the term, students are supplied with a list of books that they are expected to read.
   刚开学，学校就给学生提供了他们所需阅读的书籍目录。
   The school supplies books for the children.
   学校向孩子提供各种书籍。

Whenever she goes out with her baby, she always takes a large supply of baby food with her.

她带着孩子出门时,总会带上各种小孩所需的食品。

They used to be a leading supplier of military equipment.

他们曾经是军用设备的主要供货商。

3) Like food, all fuels **contain** energy that once stored in green plants.

contain　*v.*　to have something inside or include something as a part　包含,容纳

container　*n.*

① a hollow object, such as a box or a bottle, which can be used for holding something, especially to carry or store it　容器

② a very large metal box used for transporting goods　集装箱

containerize　*v.*　to put goods in a large metal box for transport, or to make a port, ship, etc. suitable for this method of transport　用集装箱装

containerization　*n.*　货柜运输,货柜装货;集装箱化

e.g.　*How much liquid do you think this bottle contains?*

你认为这瓶子能装多少液体呢?

I've lost a file containing a lot of important documents.

我弄丢了一个装着许多重要文件的档案袋。

a container ship/lorry

一艘集装箱船只/货车

containerized goods

用集装箱装的货物

4) If you **had traced** almost any transformation of energy back far enough, you would have found that it **began with** some change in the radiant energy from the sun.

trace

① *v.*　to find the origin of something; to discover the cause or origin of something by examining the way in which it has developed　追踪;回溯

② *n.*　a sign that something has happened or existed; an act of finding information about something electronically, or the record of the information found in this way　痕迹;追踪,探索

e.g.　*No one has yet been able to trace the source of the rumor.*

没人能追溯到谣言到底是从哪儿传来的。(谣言的源头)

The outbreak of food poisoning was traced to some contaminated shellfish.

突然爆发的食物中毒是由一些被污染的贝类引起的。(要追溯到)

The practice of giving eggs at Easter can be traced back to festivals in ancient China.

在复活节送鸡蛋的习俗可追溯到古代中国的节日习俗。

When she moved out, she left no trace of having been there.

她离开时,没留下任何她来过的痕迹。

My wallet has been missing for several days and I can't find any trace of it.
我的钱包丢了好几天了也没见它的踪迹。

He seems to have vanished without (a) trace (= No one knows where he is).
他似乎消失得无影无踪。

to begin with at the beginning of a process, event or situation; used to give the first important reason for something 以……开始；首先，第一点

e.g. There were six of us to begin with, then two people left.
开始是六个人，后来走了两个。

The school was quite a small one to begin with.
这学校最初很小。

The hotel was awful! To begin with, our room was far too small. Then we found that the shower didn't work.
这家旅店太糟糕了。首先客房太小，后来又发现淋浴器不管用。

5) If the sun were to disappear, the earth would be **plunged** into **endless** night.

plunge

① *v.* to move or fall suddenly and often a long way forward, down or into something 跳进，投入

② *n.* a sudden movement or fall forward, down or into something 跳

e.g. We ran down to the beach and plunged into the sea.
我们跑到海边，跳进了海里。

The car went out of control and plunged over the cliff.
这辆车一下失控坠入了悬崖。

I really enjoyed my plunge (= jumping in and swimming) in the pool.
我的确喜欢一跃跳入游泳池的感觉。

end

① *v.* to finish or stop, or to make something finish or stop 结束

② *n.* the point in space or time beyond which something no longer exists, or a part of something that includes this point 结束，最后

endless *adj.* never finishing or seeming never to finish 无休止的，没完没了的
endlessly *adv.*

e.g. When is your meeting due to end?
你们的会议何时结束？

Their marriage ended in 1991.
他们的婚姻是在1991年结束的。

Get to the end of the queue and wait your turn like everyone else.
排到队伍的最后面，像其他人那样等着。

Our house is the third from the end on the left.
我们的房子是在左边倒数第三间。

We used to have endless arguments about politics.
我们过去常就政治问题进行没完没了的争论。

The possibilities are endless.
可能性随时都存在。

I find myself endlessly repeating the same phrases.
我发现自己老是重复着相同的词组。

6) Even if the **brightness** of the sun were to change by only a small amount, the temperature of the earth would rise or fall sufficiently to make life impossible.

bright
① *adj.* full of light, shining 明亮的,闪光的,晴朗的
② *adj.* intelligent, (of a person) clever and quick to learn 聪明的,前途无量的

brightness *n.* 光亮,明亮;聪明

e.g. The rooms were bright and airy.
房间非常明亮,也很通风。

The lights are too bright in here—they're hurting my eyes.
这儿的光线太亮,直刺我的眼睛。

They were bright children, always asking questions.
他们是群聪明的孩子,总是爱提问题。

A bright star was shining in the East.
一颗亮晶晶的星星在东边的天空闪烁。

When she looked up her eyes were bright with tears.
她抬头的时候,眼睛里闪烁着泪花。

Look at his bright face, he is not a bit old.
看他满面春风,一点也不老。

The fresh breeze and bright sunshine quickly attracted Sophia.
清新的微风和明亮的阳光很快使索非亚着迷了。

Stars vary in brightness.
星星光亮度不同。

Her face is full of the soft brightness, which indicates a peaceful heart.
她的脸充满了柔和与愉快的表情,显示她内心平静。

7) Though the sun is 93 million miles away, it **provides** actually all the energy **for** us.

provide for sb to give someone the things they need such as money, food or clothes 为某人提供……

provide *v.* to give someone something that they need

e.g. He has a wife and two young children to provide for.
他有妻子和两个小孩要供养。

The government will be able to provide poorer families with viable social services.
政府将会为贫困家庭提供可行的社会服务。

8) For many years, scientists have been wondering why the sun can keep on **giving off** large amounts of energy.

    give sth off   to produce heat, light, a smell or a gas   发出(蒸汽、光等)

    e.g. That tiny radiator doesn't give off much heat.
    这种小型散热器发不出太多的热量。
    These gas lasers give off a continuous beam.
    这种气体激光器产生连续不断的光束。

9) It was once suggested that the sun was **actually** burning.

    actual *adj.* real; existing in fact   实际的,事实上的
    actually *adv.* in fact or really   实际上,事实上
    actuality *n.* a fact   事实

    e.g. We had estimated about 300 visitors, but the actual number was much higher.
    我们原估计有300位来宾,可实际人数却远远超过。
    The exams are in July, but the actual results (= the results themselves) don't appear until September.
    七月份举行考试,实际上,考试结果要到九月才有。
    I didn't actually see her—I just heard her voice.
    事实上我没见到她,我只和她通过话。
    So what actually happened?
    到底发生什么了?
    An imagination creation does not represent actuality but has been invented.
    想像虚构的作品,并不代表是真实的,而是被编造出来的。

10) Had this been true, the sun would have **burned** itself **out** long ago.

    burn out   烧尽(燃料),焚毁

    e.g. That factory was completely burnt out in a big fire.
    那个工厂在一场大火中被烧成了灰烬。
    His zeal will soon burn itself out.
    他的热忱很快就会冷淡下来的。
    You'll burn yourself out if you work too hard.
    假如你过分劳累,就会把精力消耗完的。

Outline:

I. **(Para. 1) Introduction**

    Most of the energy comes from one source—the sun.

II. (Para. 2–6) Body

Any transformation of energy begins with some change in the radiant energy from the sun.

1. The sun is the real source of the heat from the fuels and the mechanical energy from engines. (Para. 2)
2. The electrical energy also comes from the sun. (Para. 3)
3. The sun is the real source of the wind—the moving air. (Para. 4)
4. Examples of some transformations of energy. (Para. 5)
5. Suppose the sun disappeared, what would happen? (Para. 6)

III. (Para. 7) Conclusion

The sun provides far more energy than we have learnt how to use directly.

Text B

1) Hundreds of scientists **are making researches on** them.

   research   *n.*   [U] a detailed study of a subject, especially in order to discover (new) information or reach a (new) understanding   研究,探索

   make researches on   对……进行研究

   e.g.   *He made a research on the cause of cancer.*
   他对癌症病因进行了研究。

   It is a scientific research.
   这是一项科学研究。

   This university will have built a research laboratory by the end of the term.
   这所大学将在学期末建好一座研究实验室。

2) The atomic waste is so **powerful** that it will be a danger for centuries.

   power
   ① *n.*   strength   力量;能量
   ② *v.*   to act with great strength or in a forceful way   使……有力量

   powerful   *adj.*   having a lot of strength or force; having a very great effect   强大的,强健的;厉害的

   powerfully   *adv.*   强大地,有力地

   e.g.   *Weightlifters have tremendous power in their arms and legs.*
   举重运动员的臂膀和腿部力量都特别大。

   The economic power of many Asian countries has grown dramatically in recent years.
   许多亚洲国家的经济力量在近几年都增强了许多。

   Atomic energy powers the submarine.
   原子能供给这艘潜艇动力。

The picture quality is bad because the TV signal isn't powerful enough.
由于电视信号能量不足,使得画面质量很差。
The wine is powerful.
这酒是烈性的。
Klaus is a very powerfully-built man (= has a body with large strong muscles).
克罗斯是个体魄非常健壮的男士。

3) Some people wish that it were **safe and sound** to do so.
   safe and sound   completely safe and without injury or damage   安然无恙
   e.g. *After three days lost in the mountains, all the climbers arrived home safe and sound.*
   在山里迷路三天后,所有的登山队员都安然无恙地返回了家。
   The soldiers have returned safe and sound from the war.
   战士从战场上安然无恙地回来了。

4) We might **turn away** from the deep ocean and look at the space around our world for a place to put our atomic waste.
   turn away   to (cause to) turn in a different direction; refuse to look at, welcome, help, etc.
   转变方向;拒绝看、欢迎、帮助等
   e.g. *She turned away in horror at the sight of so much blood.*
   她一看到那么多血,害怕得掉头就走了。
   You shouldn't turn away from all your friends.
   你不应该离(避)开你所有的朋友。
   How can you turn away from a soldier who was wounded?
   你怎么能对一个受伤的战士不闻不问呢?

Outline:

I. (Para. 1) Introduction

The problem of how to deal with atomic waste is being studied by scientists and energy experts.

II. (Para. 2–9)

The only thing that we can do is to keep the waste in a place where it is harmless to people.

1. The problems of how to do with atomic waste and radioactive waste. (Para. 2–4)

2. The proposal and the method we have tried. (Para. 5)

3. The reason why it is not a complete solution to throw the atomic waste into the ocean. (Para. 6–8)

4. The wish that atomic waste could be sent in to the space. (Para. 9)

III. (Para. 10)

The situation about the earth we live on.

IV. (Para. 11) Conclusion

It is necessary that we continue the search.

Key to Unit 3

Exercises for Reading Comprehension

I. Answer the following questions.

1. Most of the energy we use comes from the sun.
2. My body gets muscular energy and heat by oxidizing food and releasing its chemical energy.
3. Yes, they are.
4. Because radiant energy from the sun was transformed into chemical energy and stored in the plants from which the fuels were made. When any fuel is burned, the chemical energy is released and changed into heat energy. In an engine, heat is transformed into mechanical energy that can be used to run machines, so the sun is also the real source of the heat from fuels and the mechanical energy from engines.
5. Generators are usually installed on dams which change the kinetic energy of water into electricity.
6. Wind has kinetic energy because of its motion.
7. No, it doesn't. It has potential energy.
8. If the sun were to disappear, the earth would be plunged into endless night. No life would be possible, and the seas and the gases of the air would freeze without the sun.
9. The sun is 93 million miles away from the sun.
10. Scientists are now quite sure that the heat and light of the sun are produced by releasing the atomic energy of certain elements.
11. The problem of how to deal with atomic waste, the harmful "used up" fuel of atomic energy, is being studied by many scientists and energy experts.
12. Hundreds of scientists are making researches on how to deal with atomic waste.
13. No, it can't.
14. No, we can't.
15. No, I don't think so. Because the cost of making the double containers and taking them to sea is very great, and it is not known how long it will be before the metal and rock containers are broken open by the force of the deep ocean currents.
16. If the containers of atomic waste should break open, the atomic waste would mix with the water and rise. There would be a great disaster that the small plants and animals that live in

the ocean water would eat the atomic waste and become poisoned. These would be eaten by large fish, and the fish eaten by men.

17. Because it would cost too much to do so.
18. Yes, it does.
19. Atomic waste is now being buried a few feet under the surface of the earth in places where it is carefully guarded and tested by specialists so that it cannot harm any living things.
20. People demand that better ways to prevent atomic waste from harming life be found.

II. Find the meanings of the words or expressions in Column (A) from those in Column (B).
1. F   2. J   3. H   4. G   5. I   6. A   7. B   8. D   9. C   10. E

III. Complete the sentences with the given expressions, and change the forms where necessary.
1. giving off
2. supplies... with
3. begins with
4. was plunged into
5. pushes against
6. provides... for
7. safe and sound
8. boiled away
9. burned out
10. turn away

IV. Complete the sentences with the given expressions, and change the forms where necessary.
1. atomic
2. muscular
3. chemical
4. radiant
5. potential
6. kinetic
7. electrical
8. light
9. mechanical
10. heat

Exercises for Language Structure

I. Fill in the blanks with verbs in their proper moods.
1. were buried, would rise
2. were to disappear, would be plunged
3. had not seen, pulled, would have been killed
4. were, would be settled
5. had been free, would have worked
6. had remembered, would have given
7. had paid, would not have succeeded
8. would have risen
9. would be

10. would have gone

II. Choose the best answer.
1. C 2. B 3. D 4. A 5. A 6. B 7. B 8. D 9. B 10. C

III. Find out which of the underlined parts in each sentence is not correct in written English.
1. C. were strict 改为 be strict
2. A. is 改为 were
3. A. weren't it 改为 were it not
4. C. would not fail 改为 would not have failed
5. B. told 改为 had told
6. A. do not travel 改为 did not travel
7. B. had 改为 have
8. A. was 改为 were
9. A. do 改为 would
10. C. can supply 改为 could supply

Practice and Improvement

Reading Skills

Speed Reading I
1. A 2. C 3. C 4. D 5. D 6. T 7. T 8. F 9. F 10. T

Speed Reading II
1. B 2. B 3. D 4. A 5. D 6. T 7. F 8. T 9. F 10. T

Cloze Procedure
1. D 2. A 3. D 4. B 5. C 6. A 7. B 8. D 9. C 10. C

Communication Function

Going to the Movies

A: Since it is Saturday today, I'm going to kill the time this evening, but I can't decide whether to watch TV or go to the movies. What's your opinion, Harry?
B: Well, if I were you, Mary, I'd go to the movies.
A: But I even don't know what is on this evening. Can you give me some advice?
B: Oh, why not ask the enquiry desk for information?

A: But many friends say there is a wonderful TV program this evening.

B: But I've heard that a terrific film "Titanic" is shown these days. It displays a ship wreck which happened about one hundred years ago with beautiful music and a romantic story. It's really a joy to see it. If I had the time, I would not lose the chance.

A: Though I'm not a film fanatic, I do enjoy the superb movies. By the way, when will the film start?

B: At 7:30. You'd better book the ticket in advance if you really want to see it.

A: Thank you for your advice.

B: I hope you will enjoy yourself this evening. See you next week.

A: Good-bye.

Listening Comprehension

I. 1. C   2. D   3. B   4. A   5. B   6. D   7. B   8. C   9. A   10. A

II. 1. C   2. B   3. C   4. A   5. D   6. A   7. C   8. D   9. B   10. B

III.
1. large amounts of
2. at the same time
3. at its current speed
4. continues to use
5. or so
6. so much energy
6. the earth's atmosphere
8. the temperature
9. the pattern
10. a frightening future

Translation Skills

I. Translate the following into English.

1. As soon as he saw the child fall into the water, he plunged into it to save him.
2. The windmill can change the kinetic energy of wind into mechanical energy.
3. The moon doesn't give off heat and light itself.
4. If the nuclear power station is watched carefully, it is safe and sound to make use of atomic energy.
5. He suggests that scientists make researches on human brains so that the new generation of computers can be made.

II. Translate the following into Chinese.

1. 太阳一旦消失,地球上就不可能有生命存在。
2. 能源专家建议我们更多地利用太阳能,以便保护环境。
3. 现在是我们必须和污染作斗争的时候了。
4. 要是科学家们早就关注能源问题就好了。

5. 现在人们大量使用石油,好像石油永远也不会停止喷流。

Writing Skills

I. Rewrite each of the sentences after the models.

Model A:

1. It is important that you (should) learn a foreign language well.
2. It is necessary that we (should) make use of solar energy.
3. It is urgent that people (should) take measures to prevent pollution.
4. It is essential that we (should) protect the environment.
5. It is necessary that scientists (should) make researches on the problems of how to deal with atomic waste.

Model B:

1. It's high time that we should prevent population explosion.
2. It's time that Tom should make preparations for the exam.
3. It's about time that the farmers went to the fields.
4. It's high time that we should form the sense of environmental protection.
5. It's about time that Prof. Wang gave us a talk on American culture.

II. Practical Writing

Learning Pact

In order to create a calm and comfortable learning environment, we, the students of Financial Class 3 Grade 2, have worked out the following learning pact after a serious discussion:

1. Plan the time carefully. Make a list of the terminal task, and then make a timetable.

2. Keep the classroom clean and tidy and study seriously and independently in scheduled time.

3. Study regularly, preview the textbooks before class and review the lessons after class.

4. Listen to the lectures attentively in class, and take notes to remember what the teachers have taught.

5. Finish assignments in time and develop a good attitude towards the tests.

All Students of Financial Class 3, Grade 2

March 1, 2005

Tape Scripts for Listening Comprehension

I. Directions: *In this section you will hear 10 statements. Each statement will be read only once. Then there will be a pause. During the pause, you must read the four choices marked A, B, C and D, and decide which is closest in meaning to the sentence you have just heard, and then choose the corresponding letter.*

1. I bought this 200-dollar TV set for 160 dollars.
2. I'm not young any more.
3. Fred sits there reading though the radio is on.
4. The cup with a blue handle is in the white box.
5. Stella is playing tennis and Frank is too.
6. Pax prefers swimming to ball games.
7. He thought cooking was pleasant.
8. As one of four directors of the company Jack often attended important meetings.
9. I remember telling you about her.
10. He is apparently a very old man, but in fact he is only fifty.

II. Directions: *In this section, you will hear 10 short conversations. At the end of each conversation, a question will be asked about what was said. The conversation and the question will be spoken only one time. After each question, there will be a pause. During the pause, you must read the four choices marked A, B, C and D, and decide which the best answer is, and then choose the corresponding letter.*

1. W: Do you have Susan's number in California?
   M: Not yet. She promised she'd send it to me as soon as she had a phone.
   Q: What do you learn from this talk?
2. M: I'd like five apples, a dozen eggs, and a birthday cake.
   W: Do you want the cake decorated?
   Q: Where does this conversation take place?
3. W: Sam always puts things off until the last minute.
   M: He'd better hurry if he wants to hand in his homework before Friday.
   Q: What do we learn about Sam?
4. W: Peter should run for office.
   M: He's organized and a good speaker.
   Q: What do they think about Peter?
5. M: The baby crying next door kept me up all night.
   W: She must be ill.
   Q: What happened to the man?

6. M: What will you do after graduation?
   W: I don't know whether or not to go out on my own or work for a large company.
   Q: What is one of the woman's choices?
7. W: Where can I write you this summer?
   M: While I'm at summer school in New York, you can write me at my brother's address.
   Q: Where can the woman write the man?
8. M: Did you make a reservation on the 7: 00 flight?
   W: I thought you wanted to take the 6: 00. It's too late to change now.
   Q: What happened to the woman?
9. M: I wish you had told me your holiday plans sooner.
   W: I'm sorry. I thought you know I go to my parents' country house each August.
   Q: Why is the man upset?
10. W: If you are in a hurry you can take the subway. If you want to look round, take a bus.
    M: Actually, I don't have to be at the meeting before noon.
    Q: What will the man probably do?

III. Directions: *In this section you will hear a passage of about 90 words three times. There are about 20 words missing. First, you will hear the whole passage from the beginning to the end just to get a general idea about it. Then, in the second reading, write down the missing words during the pauses. You can check what you have written when the passage is read to you once again without the pauses.*

Many scientists are optimistic that new ways of generating **large amounts of** energy will be successfully developed, but **at the same time** they fear consequences. If the world population goes on increasing **at its current speed**, and each individual **continues to use** more energy every year, we may, in 50 years **or so**, be burning up **so much energy** that we may pollute **the earth's atmosphere**. By raising **the temperature** of the atmosphere, we could melt the Arctic and Antarctic ice-caps and change **the pattern** of vegetable and animal life throughout the world—**a frightening future**!

Online Resources:

1. http://www.etslan.com/
2. http://www.theunion.com/article/20050825/OPINION/108250083/0/FRONTPAGE
3. http://www.rednova.com/news/display/?id=219347&source=r_science
4. http://www.bizjournals.com/portland/stories/2005/08/22/daily37.html?from_rss=1
5. http://biz.yahoo.com/bw/050823/235197.html?.v=1

Text Translation for Reference

第三单元 能源的观念就是未来的观念

A 课文

什么是我们主要的能源?

我们使用的绝大多数能量其实就一个源头。如果你考虑到一些重要的能量转换,你便会明白为什么这么说。你的身体通过食物的氧化和释放化学能量,获得肌肉的能量和热量,这种能氧化的食物是通过绿色植物的光合作用形成,来自太阳的辐射能转化成化学能量,贮藏在食物中。因此太阳就是你体内肌肉能量和热量的真正来源。

有些机器是由肌肉能驱动的,但是大多数机器是由机械能驱动的,这种能量通常由燃烧某种燃料的引擎所提供。像食物一样,所有燃料都包含着曾经贮藏于绿色植物中的能量。煤是由数百万年以前大型蕨类植物和其他绿色植物的死体形成的,汽油、煤油和燃油都是从石油当中提炼成的。而石油可能是由数百万年前的小型植物或者小型食草动物形成的。来自太阳的辐射能被转换成化学能,并贮藏于形成燃料的植物中。因此,当燃料燃烧时,化学能得以释放,进而转变成热能。在引擎中,热量被转换成运转机器的机械能,因此,太阳同样是热能(来自于燃料)和机械能(来自于引擎)的真正来源。

电风扇、真空吸尘器、电冰箱、空调和许多其他设备都是由电动机带动的。电动机将电能转变为机械能,而电能是从发电站经导线传输的。发电站安装有使电流经导线的发电机,由此,发电机将机械能转变为电能。机械能通常是由燃烧燃料的引擎来提供,因此你能明白驱动发动机的电能实际上来自于太阳。

然而,有些发电机是由来自水车或风车的机械能带动的。大家知道风是一种流动的空气,像流动的水一样,空气因为流动而具有动能。太阳也是这种动能的真正来源。当太阳普照大地,辐射能被转换成热能,这时热量使空气膨胀,因而空气较轻。刮风是因为某处的暖空气强于另一地方的暖空气。地心引力以更大的力量拉低较冷重的空气,当这较冷重的空气沉到地面,它就推开较轻暖的气体,于是较轻暖的空气被强力向外和向上推动,沿着地球运动的气流就形成了风。

当太阳照在河流、湖畔和海洋的水面上,辐射能也能被转换成热能。热能将水转换成水蒸气,风又将水蒸气带到高空。水蒸气由于上升受地心引力的作用而具有势能。当水蒸气充分冷却时,就会形成雨或雪降落在大地上,然后雨水或融化的雪水流下山岗,又流向海洋,水蒸气的势能被转换成流水的动能。因此,不管是引擎、水车,还是风车都能用来提供机械能,而太阳就是发电机电能的真正来源。如果你充分探索了能量的所有转换形式,你会发现能量的转换是由太阳辐射能变化开始的。

太阳是个巨大的球状物,非常热,有着灼热的气体。太阳一旦消失,地球将会陷入无穷无尽的黑夜之中。没有太阳,生命绝不可能存在,甚至大海和大气层中的气体也会凝固。即使太阳的亮度稍有一点变化，地球的温度也会随之升高或降低到足以使生命不能延续下去的地步。

虽然太阳离我们有9300万英里之遥，但实际上提供了我们所有的能量。实际上，它所提供的能量远远超过我们已知如何直接利用的能量。照射在地球上三分钟的辐射能就足以提供我们一年所需的所有能量，然而仅有一少部分的太阳能量到达了地球，大部分的能量辐射到太空去了。多年来科学家一直想知道太阳是怎样持续不断地释放出巨大能量的。曾有人认为太阳实际上是在燃烧，假如这是真的，太阳早就燃烧尽了。科学家现在颇为相信太阳的光和热是由某些元素释放的原子能产生的。

B 课文

如何处理原子废料？

许多科学家和能源专家正在研究如何处理原子废料——这一有害的、用过的原子能燃料。

大型原子能反应堆能产生巨大的能量，与此同时也产生了有害的放射性元素。原子废料威力如此强大，以至于它产生的危险将持续几个世纪。如何处理原子废料？将其置于什么地方才能对人类不产生危害呢？应该是我们解决这一问题的时候了。数以百计的科学家正在对此进行研究。

你会怎样处理放射性的原子废料呢？将它与水混和倒入海洋？假如你生活在水边，你就不会这么做了。假如你把一小盒子原子废料扔进一片100多英里长，约15英里宽的水域，在不到24小时内，用一个特殊的仪器，就可在该水域的任何地方监测到这少量的原子废料。这表明了怎样处理原子废料这一问题的深度和广度。

原子废料不能被燃烧，被蒸发，或者与其他物质混合而变得无害。我们不是在研究可以被摧毁的物质，我们是在尝试摧毁能量，而这是不可能的。我们惟一可做的就是将废料置于一个对人类无害的地方。

另一个方案就是我们将原子废料扔入海洋。实际上这个方案已经尝试过了。原子废料被置于金属桶里，然后将金属桶放进岩石一般厚实的容器。这些容器被带到海洋的深处，然后投下。有些人希望这样做能安全无恙，然而，由于各种各样的原因，将原子废料投入大海并不是一个能彻底解决问题的办法。

首先，制造双层的容器并将它们运送到海边的费用是十分昂贵的；第二，我们不知道这个金属和岩石的容器多久以后会因为深海水流的外力而破裂。当原子废料泄漏流进深海，这是多么危险的事情啊！

大多数科学家都认为原子废料是有害的，他们也知道，在海洋数千英尺以下的深层海水会不断上升，最后和表层海水混和在一起，但他们不知道要花多长时间才形成这种混和。

假如装有原子废料的容器破裂，原子废料就会与海水混合，并浮升到海面。生活在海里的小型动植物吃下原子废料，然后中毒，这将是一场巨大的灾难。因为这些小型动植物会被大鱼吞食，而大鱼又会被人类食用。所以把原子废料装入桶内，投进大海不是解决问题的最好方法。

我们不妨避开大洋深处,看看我们地球周围的空间,从而找出一个贮放原子废料的场所。有人希望原子废料可以放在导弹上发射到远离我们地球的地方去。这个解决方法听起来不那么难,也能做到,但是花费高昂。

　　那么我们赖以生存的地球呢?原子废料通常是一种液体,不能泼洒到地面。假如这样做了,这种液体就会很快扩散,渗入地表,然后接触水源、动植物和人群。你也许会建议把原子废料放进桶里埋入地下。那里没有海洋水流,不会导致桶的破裂,但是你必须记住原子废料是一种能量,它能产生热量。假如它被埋在地底下,温度会上升很高,桶将会破裂。

　　实际上原子废料如今一直被埋藏在地表数英尺之下,并受到专家们细心的看护和监测,以防它们损害生物。然而,把原子废料埋藏于地下,就像把它投进大海,并不是最终的解决方法。人类需要找出更好的方法来防止原子废料损害生物。我们有必要继续探寻。

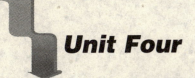

Unit Four

THE CLONING TECHNOLOGY

Objective

By the end of this unit, the learners are required to grasp the following:

I. Key Words and Phrases

1. Words:

   clone, cloned, cloning
   predict, predictable, unpredictable
   trouble, troublesome, troublesomely
   gene, genetic, genetics, geneticist
   vary, variable, various, variety, variability

2. Phrases:

   fight against stamp out suffer from be applied to
   clean up a wide variety of aim to on the other hand
   response to result in

II. Language Structure

   The Agreement

III. Practice and Improvement

   Reading Skills: Speed Reading and Cloze Procedure
   Speaking Skills: Showing Warnings and Commands
   Listening Skills: Sound Recognition, Dialogues, and Spot Dictation
   Translation Skills: Phrases and the Agreement
   Writing Skills: Sentence Patterns and Posters

Word Usage

Reading Selection

Text A

1) Their work **aims** to find practical **applications** for cloning that produce advances in medicine, biological research, and industry.

   aim　*v.*　目的在于, 旨在, 志在
   e.g.　*I aim to be a millionaire by the time I'm 35.*
   　　　我的目标是35岁成为百万富翁。

   application　*n.*　a way in which something can be used for a particular purpose　应用
   e.g.　*"Freedom" is a word of wide application.*
   　　　"自由"一词可用于多种场合。

   apply　*v.*　to make use of something or use it for a practical purpose　运用, 应用
   e.g.　*He wants a job in which he can apply his foreign languages.*
   　　　他想干一份能用得上他的外语能力的工作。
   　　　Students should learn to apply a theory to practice.
   　　　学生应该学会把理论应用于实践。

   applicable　*adj.*　affecting or relating to a person or thing　生效的
   e.g.　*This law is only applicable to companies employing more than five people.*
   　　　这项法律只适用于五人以上的公司。
   　　　The new qualifications are applicable to all European countries.
   　　　这些新的限制适用于欧洲的所有国家。

2) These early forms of cloning and breeding were slow and sometimes **unpredictable**.

   unpredictable　*adj.*　tending to change suddenly and without reason and therefore cannot be predicted or depended on　不可预知的
   e.g.　*The weather there can be a bit unpredictable—one minute it's blue skies and the next minute it's pouring down.*
   　　　那儿的天气有点不可预测,这一刻还蓝蓝的天,一会儿就倾盆大雨了。

   predict　请参阅第一单元课文 B 的词语学习。

   predictable　*adj.*　Something which is predictable happens in a way or at a time which you know about before it happens.　可预测的, 可预言的
   e.g.　*The results are not predictable since the system cannot ensure that data will be processed correctly.*
   　　　由于系统不能保证数据的正确处理,其结果是不可预测的。

3) Scientists **combine** genetic engineering **with** cloning to quickly and inexpensively **produce thousands of** plants with a desired characteristic.

    combine *v.* to (cause to) exist together, or join together to make a single thing or group 使联合,结合

    e.g. We must combine theory with practice.
         我们必须把理论和实践结合起来。

         Sickness, combined with (= together with) terrible weather, contrived to ruin the trip.
         身体不舒服,加之糟糕的天气,使我们的旅游成了泡影。

    thousands of 数以千计的,大量的,成千上万的
         相类似的表达法   hundreds of, millions of

    e.g. Thousands of people go to the seaside every year.
         每年都有许多的人到海边。

         Thousands of letters are never delivered because the addresses are incorrect.
         由于地址不对,许多的信件都没法投递。

produce *v.*
① to make something or bring something into existence   出产,制造
② When animals produce young, they give birth to them.   生产

    e.g. France produces a great deal of wine for export.
         法国生产红葡萄酒以出口。

         Red blood cells are produced in the bone marrow.
         红血球是在骨髓里产生的。

         Wealth may not produce civilization, but civilization produce money.
         财富未必创造文明,文明却能带来金钱。

         Our cat produced four kittens during the course of the night.
         我们的猫一夜就产了四个小猫咪。

producer *n.* a company, country or person that provides goods, especially those which are produced by an industrial process or grown or obtained through farming, usually in large amounts 生产者,制造者(人、国、商)

    e.g. Australia is one of the world's main producers of wool.
         澳大利亚是世界上羊毛的主要生产国之一。

         The company is a major car producer.
         这个公司是一个大的汽车制造(生产)厂商。

product *n.* something that is made to be sold, usually something that is produced by an industrial processor, less commonly; something that is grown or obtained through farming 产品,产物

    e.g. They do a range of skin-care products.
         他们在做一系列护肤产品。

         I'm trying to cut down on daily products.
         我在试图削减日常用品的开支。

reproduce   *v.*

① When living things reproduce, they produce young.   繁殖,再生
② to produce a copy of something, or to be copied in a production process   复制

e.g.   *These plants can reproduce sexually and asexually.*
这些植物可以有性繁殖,也可以无性繁殖。

They said the printing was too faint to reproduce well.
他们说这画太模糊,没法复制。

4) Cloning techniques can also **be applied to** animals.

be applied to   适用于,应用于

e.g.   *Scientific discoveries are often applied to industrial production methods.*
科学的发现经常应用于改进工业生产方式。

Students should apply a theory to practice.
学生应该把理论应用于实践。

5) Many people **fight against** the creation and cloning of genetically modified plants.

fight against   对抗,与……斗争

e.g.   *We will fight against the enemy.*
我们将与敌人作战。

We are all brothers in the same fight against injustice.
在共同反对非正义行为的斗争中,我们都是兄弟。

We must all fight against cruelty and unfairness.
我们都应该反对残忍和不公平的事。

6) Animal cloning, **on the other hand**, stirs heartfelt controversy.

on the other hand   另一方面

e.g.   *On the one hand I'd like a job which pays more, but on the other hand I enjoy the work I'm doing at the moment.*
一方面我愿意找一份挣钱多的工作,另一方面我又喜欢现在的这份工作。

He is clever, but on the other hand, he makes many mistakes.
他很聪明,可另一方面他常出错。

7) This could **result in** the development of cloned animals or humans with serious defects.

result in sth   to cause a particular situation to happen   导致,造成

e.g.   *The fire resulted in damage to their property.*
这场火灾给他们财产造成了损失。

Acting before thinking always results in failure.
做事不先考虑总会导致失败。

The accident resulted in the death of two people.
这场意外事故造成两人死亡。

Outline:

I. (Para. 1) Introduction

Cloning can create a copy of living matter, and many organisms in nature reproduce by cloning.

II. (Para. 2)

The development of cloning

1. Farmers started cloning plants thousands of years ago in simple ways.
2. Scientists developed genetic engineering by the late 20th century.

III. (Para. 3–5)

Cloning techniques can be used in many fields and for many purposes.

1. They can be used to reproduce the genetically modified animals. (Para. 3)
2. Industry also uses cloning technology. (Para. 4)
3. Cloning promises great advances in medicine. (Para. 5)

IV. (Para. 6–7) Conclusion

The future of cloning remains uncertain because of so much controversy.

1. Many people fight against the creation and cloning of genetically modified plants. (Para. 6)
2. Animal cloning stirs heartfelt controversy. (Para. 7)

Text B

1) Since the cloning of Dolly the sheep in 1996, scientists have cloned **a wide variety of** mammals from adult cells... (Para. 1)

a wide variety of 各种各样的,许多的

e.g. *The library had a wide variety of books.*
图书馆里有各种各样的书籍。

The hotel offers its guests a wide variety of amusements.
这个旅馆为住客提供了各种各样的娱乐活动。

2) Somatic nuclear transfer is **inefficient**—few cloned embryos survive through birth.

efficiency *n.* 效率,功能

e.g. *Friction lowers the efficiency of a machine.*
摩擦降低机器的效率。

efficient *adj.* 有效率的

e.g. *She's very efficient.*
她办事干净利落。

He was efficient in his work.
他工作效率高。

inefficient *adj.* 效率低的,效率差的,无能的

e.g. *He is an inefficient worker.*
他是个不称职的工人。

The government refuses to prop up inefficient industries.
政府拒绝补贴效益不佳的行业。

inefficiently *adv.*

e.g. *The hotel is inefficiently run.*
这旅店经营不善。

You can't afford to run businesses inefficiently in this day and age.
在现今,经营商店无能是不行的。

3) Scientists **implanted** 371 embryos **into** surrogate mothers...

plant *v.* (常与 in, into 连用)灌输,注入,植入

e.g. *He always implants hope in the mind.*
他总是怀抱希望。

How do you implant good manners in your children?
你是怎样培养儿女们懂礼貌、守规矩的呢?

to implant microorganisms or infectious material into (a culture medium)
菌体培养把微生物或传染性物质植入(培养基)

4) Healthy plant and animal populations in the wild maintain **genetic** diversity—a wide variety of **genes** in different combination—through sexual reproduction.

gene *n.* [遗传]因子,[遗传]基因

e.g. *Scientists developed techniques for altering genes or combinations of genes in an organism.*
科学工作者研制出了在活体中转化基因,或将基因结合的技术。

genetic *adj.* 遗传的,起源的,基因的

e.g. *Genetic engineering stands out as a significant twentieth-century event because it may allow us to end disease, hunger, and pollution.*
基因工程成为20世纪的重大事件是因为它可能让我们结束疾病、饥饿和污染。

genetics *n.* 遗传学

geneticist *n.* 遗传学者

e.g. *Also in the 1980s, geneticists implant a human-growth hormone gene into mice,...*
同样,在20世纪80年代,科学家将人体增长的荷尔蒙基因注入老鼠体内,……

5) As Dolly the sheep aged, scientists reported that she **prematurely** developed arthritis.

mature

① *v.* to become more developed mentally and emotionally and behave in a responsible way
成熟

② *adj.* completely grown physically 成熟的

e.g. *Girls are said to mature faster than boys.*
人们都说女孩比男孩成熟的快一些。

He matured a lot while he was at college.
在大学期间,他成熟了许多。

His character was matured by age.
他的性格因年龄而成熟。

He's a mature man who can make his own decisions.
他是个成年人,会自己做出决定。

maturely   *adv.*   in a mature way   成熟地,充分地

maturity   *n.*   [U] the quality of behaving mentally and emotionally like an adult   成熟

e.g. *This job calls for a man with a great deal of maturity.*
这项工作要求一个富有经验的人来干。

premature   *adj.*   早熟的,未成熟的

e.g. *I had been a little too premature in coming to this conclusion.*
做出这样的结论,我有点太草率。

prematurely   *adv.*   早熟地

e.g. *Their baby was born prematurely and weighed only 1 kilogram.*
他们的小孩早产,才1公斤重。

His stressful job made him go prematurely grey (= made his hair turn grey at a young age).
他工作的压力使得他的头发过早地白了。

6) A single virus could **wipe out** these crops.

wipe out   消灭,毁灭

e.g. *The campaign to wipe out illiteracy launched out with great vigor.*
扫盲运动生气勃勃地展开了。

You should wipe out the unpleasant memo.
你应抹掉那不快的回忆。

7) Similarly, if every cow in the herd came from a single clone, one disease could potentially **stamp out** the entire herd.

stamp out   to get rid of something that is wrong or harmful   毁掉,根除,废止

e.g. *It is difficult to stamp out all the crimes.*
很难把所有的犯罪都消除掉。

The doctors are trying to stamp out the plague by using new method.
医生们在试着用新的方法消灭这种瘟疫。

8) Moreover, scientists could clone a large number of animals that **suffer from** a human disease...

suffer from   to experience physical or mental pain   忍受,遭受

e.g. *His parents suffered from cold and hunger in winter before liberation.*
解放前,他的父母冬天总是饥寒交迫。
She's been suffering from (= been ill with) cancer for two years.
两年来,她一直遭受着癌症的折磨。

9) Some cloned animals such as sheep and pigs live for years, and scientists could use these animals to evaluate their long-term **response to** drug treatment.
response to 对……反应
e.g. *They make a quick response to my inquiry.*
他们对我的询问很快作了答复。

Summary:

Even though scientists have achieved some remarkable advances in animals cloning, drawbacks remain. Early studies provide questionable results about the health of cloning animals. While healthy plant and animal populations in the wild maintain genetic diversity through sexual reproduction, large populations of cloned plants or animals may lack genetic diversity. Anyhow, scientists believe that one day cloning will advance agricultural practices and medicine, and even prevent the extinction of endangered animals.

Key to Unit 4

Exercises for Reading Comprehension

I. Answer the following questions.
1. Cloning is creating a copy of living matter, such as a cell or organism. The copies produced through cloning have identical genetic makeup and are known as clones.
2. Their work aims to find practical applications for cloning that will produce advances in medicine, biological research, and industry.
3. Farmers started cloning plants thousands of years ago in simple ways, such as taking a cutting of a plant and letting it root to make another plant. Early farmers also devised breeding techniques to reproduce plants with such characteristics as faster growth, larger seeds, or sweeter fruits. They combined these breeding techniques with cloning to produce many plants with desired traits.
4. By the late 20th century.
5. Yes, they can.
6. Scientists hope to bolster populations of endangered species by cloning members from existing populations in the near future.

7. Little controversy ever surrounded plant cloning. In fact, few people even think of making plants from cuttings as cloning at all, but it is. Many people fight against the creation and cloning of genetically modified plants.

8. No, they don't. Critics argue that the science of cloning is in its infancy and, in order to achieve success mistakes may be made along the way.

9. Opponents to human cloning argue that without proper regulation, cloning could result in such questionable practices as designing babies with chosen genetic qualities so that they are more athletic, beautiful, or intelligent. Others fear that cloning tampers with God's will.

10. No, it doesn't. As a result of so much controversy, the future of cloning remains uncertain.

11. In 1996.

12. Yes, they do.

13. In experiments to create the first cloned rabbits in 2001, scientists implanted 371 embryos into surrogate mothers, but only six cloned rabbits were born.

14. Perhaps more troublesome, early studies provide questionable results about the health of animals cloned using somatic cell nuclear transfer.

15. Genetic diversity can make a population more resistant to disease and environmental changes.

16. Despite these drawbacks, scientists believe that animal cloning will one day advance agricultural practices and medicine, and even prevent the extinction of endangered animals.

17. In agriculture, cloned cattle could produce a higher yield of meat or milk.

18. The pharmaceutical industry already uses cloned animals to produce drugs for human use.

19. One day pharmaceutical firms may clone large populations of genetically modified animals to quickly and inexpensively derive this protein for use in drug products.

20. Cloned animals could also improve laboratory experiments. Researchers could create many genetically identical animals to reduce the variability in a sample population used in experiments, making it easier for scientists to evaluate disease.

II. Find the meanings of the words or expressions in Column (A) from those in Column (B).
1. C   2. E   3. G   4. H   5. F   6. A   7. I   8. J   9. D   10. B

III. Complete the sentences with the given expressions, and change the forms where necessary.
1. aimed to   2. clean up
3. on the other hand   4. fight against
5. a wide variety of   6. stamped out
7. suffered from   8. resulted in
9. be applied to   10. response to

IV. Fill in the blanks with the words listed below, and be sure to use appropriate verb forms and appropriate singular and plural forms for nouns.
1. trouble, troublesome, troublesomely   2. variable, variability

3. clone, cloned, cloning
4. genetics, geneticist, genetic, gene
5. predict, predictable, unpredictable

V. **Complete the following passage by using appropriate words listed below, and be sure to use singular or plural forms for nouns.**
1. cloning
2. cell
3. Thousands of
4. breeding
5. characteristics
6. be applied to
7. bolster
8. result in
9. defects
10. In spite of

Exercises for Language Structure

I. **Fill in the blanks with the correct number forms of the given verbs.**
1. come
2. are
3. are
4. is
5. are... are
6. was
7. comes
8. was
9. calls
10. is

II. **Revise the following sentences.**
1. The physicist could remember what the formulae were.
2. Although we were laid off, we think, there were still scads of opportunities for all of us.
3. The atmosphere is as much a part of the earth as are its soils and the water of its lakes, rivers and oceans.
4. No bread eaten by man is so sweet as that earned by his own labor.
5. The university offers much more courses than has been expected.
6. No administrator or supervisor can enter a classroom unless he is invited by the teacher.
7. More than one leading cadre was involved in the bride case.
8. The number of books missing from the city library is quite large.
9. Two hours is enough for students to finish the examination paper.
10. The deceased was her husband, who left a large sum of money to her.

III. **Choose the best answer.**
1. A 2. C 3. B 4. D 5. B 6. C 7. A 8. B 9. A 10. C

IV. **Find out which of the underlined parts in each sentence is not correct in written English.**
1. D. its 改为 his
2. B. these 改为 those
3. A. are 改为 is
4. C. doesn't 改为 don't

5. D. oneself 改为 ourselves
6. D. rest 改为 rests
7. B. has 改为 have
8. C. remains 改为 remain
9. C. is 改为 am
10. C. goes 改为 go

Practice and Improvement

Reading Skills

Speed Reading I
1. B   2. B   3. C   4. C   5. A   6. T   7. F   8. T   9. F   10. T

Speed Reading II
1. C   2. B   3. B   4. D   5. A   6. F   7. F   8. T   9. T   10. F

Cloze Procedure
1. C   2. B   3. A   4. C   5. B   6. D   7. A   8. B   9. D   10. C

Communication Function

II. Conversation

Showing Warnings and Commands

A: What's the matter with you, Jim? You look pale.
B: I feel awful today. I didn't get any sleep last night.
A: What happened?
B: I had pains in my stomach.
A: What have you been eating?
B: Well, let me see. I dined out with Jack yesterday evening. Then I came home and watched TV. Then I ate some potato chips, a bar of chocolate, some chestnuts and...
A: That's enough. Anyone would get pains in the stomach after eating that much. Remember to take a tablet after dinner. It will help your digestion. And mind you, don't eat so much fried food and junk food.

Listening Comprehension

I. 1. B   2. A   3. A   4. B   5. A   6. A   7. B   8. A   9. B   10. B

II. 1. C   2. B   3. B   4. D   5. A   6. A   7. C   8. C   9. D   10. B

III.
1. cloning
2. root
3. breeding
4. characteristics
5. traits
6. unpredictable
7. genetic
8. genes
9. inexpensively
10. desired

Translation Skills

I. Translate the following into English.
1. Cloning techniques can also be applied to animals.
2. From a human perspective, cloning promises great advances in medicine.
3. Scientists could clone a large number of animals that suffer from a human disease.
4. There is more than one answer to your question.
6. Both Linda and Nancy are very confident of their future.

II. Translate the following into Chinese.
1. 早在几千年前,农民就开始运用简易的方法克隆植物了。
2. 科学家们相信在将来的某一天克隆动物能够促进农业技术和医学的发展。
3. 另一方面,大量的克隆动物和植物都有可能缺乏遗传的多样性。
4. 这两个女孩都没有超过18岁。
5. 我说的话与你毫无关系。

Writing Skills

I. Revise the following sentences.
1. The government is doing its best to boost production.
2. The British police have only very limited powers.
3. *The New York Times* is published daily.
4. At the bottom of the hill there is a dangerous crossroad.
5. Neither the Kansas coach nor the players were confident of victory.
6. Every change of season, every change of weather, indeed, every hour of the day, produces some change in magical hues and shapes of these mountains.
7. John, rather than his roommates, is to be blamed.
8. Many a boy was disappointed after seeing the film.
9. A total of 60,000 new bicycles were registered this month.
10. Why he entered the house and how he managed to get out of it without being seen by people remain a mystery to us all.

II. Practical Writing

> **Poster**
>
> **Friendly Basketball Match**
>
>   Under the auspices of the Recreational and Physical Culture Department of the Students' Union, a friendly basketball match will be held between the Hunan Business Vocational College Woman Basketball Team and ours in the college gymnasium on Friday, April 22, 2005, at 4:00 p.m.
>
>   All are warmly welcome to be present at the match to cheer the players.
>
> The Recreational and Physical Culture Department
of the Students' Union
>
> Wednesday, April 20, 2005

Tape Scripts for Listening Comprehension

I. Directions: *Listen to the following sentences. Choose which word the speaker or the tape says. Tick the right word.*

1. Scientists use cloning techniques in the laboratory to create copies of cells or organisms with valuable **traits**.
2. Cloning, creating a copy of living matter, such as a **cell** or organism.
3. The copies produced through cloning have **identical** genetic makeup and are known as clones.
4. Cloning techniques can also be **applied** to animals.
5. In the near future scientists hope to **bolster** populations of endangered species.
6. The process fuels a **fiery** battle.
7. Somatic cell nuclear transfer is **inefficient**.
8. Scientists implanted **371** embryos into surrogate mothers, but only six cloned rabbits were born.
9. A single **virus** could wipe out these crops.
10. If every cow in a herd came from a single clone, one disease could potentially stamp out the entire **herd**.

II. Directions: *In this section, you will hear 10 short conversations. At the end of each conversation, a question will be asked about what was said. The conversation and the question will be spoken only one time. After each question, there will be a pause. During the pause, you must read the four choices marked A, B, C and D, and decide which the best answer is, and then choose the corresponding letter.*

1. M: Are you still planning to rent a house?
   W: Yes, but not until I get back from my winter vacation.
   Q: What will the woman do first?

2. M: There's an advertisement here for a part-time teacher. Working hours are flexible and salary is not bad.
   W: What's the telephone number? I'll call and find out if I can go for an interview.
   Q: What is the woman interested in?

3. M: Did you ask Richard if he'd like to come to the party on Friday evening?
   W: I've been dialing his number all day but keep a busy signal.
   Q: Will Richard come to the party?

4. W: Is this Accounts Department? I'd like to speak to the manager.
   M: Hold the line, please. I'll get Mr. Wong immediately.
   Q: What does Mr. Wong do?

5. W: Have you seen the boy in blue?
   M: Yes, he ran out the front door a moment ago.
   Q: What do we learn about the boy?

6. W: Would you mind bringing me the letter in the mailbox?
   M: Of course not.
   Q: What does the man mean?

7. M: If I had stopped the old lady from going alone, the accident wouldn't have happened.
   W: I don't think you're to be blamed for her actions.
   Q: What does the man mean?

8. W: I wonder if we should cancel our plan.
   M: No one of us hesitated to go out on a picnic in such bad weather.
   Q: What do we learn from this conversation?

9. M: Have you checked the front gate yet?
   W: I'm sure it's secure.
   Q: What does the woman say about the gate?

10. M: What can I do for you?
    W: Have you got any shampoo for greasy hair?
    M: I'll check, but I think we only have it for dry.
    Q: Where does this conversation probably take place?

III. **Directions:** *In this section you will hear a passage of about 90 words three times. There are about 20 words missing. First, you will hear the whole passage from the beginning to the end just to get a general idea about it. Then, in the second reading, write down the missing words during the pauses. You can check what you have written when the passage is read to you once again without the pauses.*

Farmers started **cloning** plants thousands of years ago in simple ways, such as taking a cutting of a plant and letting it **root** to make another plant. Early farmers also devised **breeding** techniques to reproduce plants with such **characteristics** as faster growth, larger seeds, or sweeter fruits. They combined these breeding techniques with cloning to produce many plants with desired **traits**. These early forms of cloning and breeding were slow and sometimes **unpredictable**. By the late 20th century scientists developed **genetic** engineering, in which they manipulate DNA, the genetic material of living things, to more precisely modify a plant's **genes**. Scientists combine genetic engineering with cloning to quickly and **inexpensively** produce thousands of plants with a **desired** characteristic.

Online Resources:

1. http://www.dailynews.lk/2005/08/27/fea01.htm
2. http://www.timesleader.com/mld/timesleader/news/nation/12462148.htm
3. http://news.yahoo.com/news?tmpl=story&u=/afp/20050825/hl_afp/healthcloneskorea
4. http://au.news.yahoo.com/050826/2/vofe.html
5. http://www.sabcnews.com/sci_tech/science/0,2172,110069,00.html

Text Translation for Reference

第四单元 克隆技术

A 课文

克隆的概述

克隆是指对活质的复制,比如说对一个细胞或者一个有机体。通过克隆复制的物质具有同一遗传结构,因此被称为克隆物。自然界很多有机体是通过克隆再生的。科学家们利用克隆技术在实验室制作出有价值的细胞或有机体的复制品,他们研究的目的就是想要找到克隆在实践中的应用,以推动药物、生物研究以及工业的发展。

在数千年前农民便用简单方法开始克隆植物,比如拿一株植物的插枝,让它生根长成另一株植物。早期的农民还发明了育种技术来再生植物,使之具有生长更快、种子更大或果实更甜的特性。他们把这些育种技术和克隆联合在一起,产生了许多带有预期性的植物。这些早期的克隆和育种形式效果很慢,有时还不可预知。到了20世纪末科学家开发了遗传工程,熟练掌握了DNA这一生物的遗传物质,由此更精确地将一株植物的基因进行变更。科学家把遗传工程和克隆联合在一起,快速廉价地生产出数以千计的具有预期特性的植物。

克隆技术也可以应用于动物,科学家研制出因基因变异而具有新特性的动物,比如抗病的能力,他们还利用克隆技术繁殖基因变异的动物。未来几年里,科学家希望从现存的物种数量中通过克隆成员,增加濒临灭绝物种的数量。有朝一日科学家甚至可以从保存的标本中通过克隆细胞,使灭绝的物种复活。

工业同样需要使用克隆技术,举例来说,有的细菌吃的是一些有毒物质,诸如汽油或者工业化学物等一些常见的污染物。这些细菌能够被克隆出大量的具有清理环境污染物能力的细菌。同样,人们能够利用克隆动物制造各种各样的成分用于许多商品,比如蛋白质。

从人类的观点来看,最重要的是克隆能够大大促进医学的发展。科学家已经将含有人类基因的DNA碎片作为一个血液凝块的蛋白质置入一只羊的细胞中,通过克隆技术,科学家已经生产出新型的羊种,其羊奶中含有血液凝块混乱的血友病人所必需的蛋白质。在不久的将来,研究人员希望使用克隆培育出患有人类疾病的动物,并利用这些克隆动物测试出对人类安全有效的新型治疗方法。生物医学家希望从病人体内获取细胞,通过基因改变它们,然后克隆变异的细胞,培养病人所需要的细胞以使他们重获健康。一些科学家甚至想像总有一天克隆会成为器官移植过程中的一部分。

尽管克隆存在着现时和潜在的好处,可整个过程却导致了异常激烈的论战。围绕着植物克隆的争论很少。实际上,很少有人想到,用插枝的技术再造植物的过程是克隆,可这种做法的确就是克隆。很多人反对这种创造物以及通过基因变异制出的植物的克隆,但是这个担忧一般只涉及植物DNA的处置,而并非克隆的整个过程。

另一方面,动物克隆却激起了真心真意的论战。批评家认为克隆科学还处于初始阶段,为了获取成功,研制过程中少不了出错,这样会导致开发出有严重缺陷的克隆动物或人类。反对人类克隆的人认为没有适当的管理规章,克隆将导致一些有问题的实验,例如用选择性的基因质量来设计婴儿,使之更健康、更漂亮或更聪明。另一些人担心克隆篡改了上帝的意愿。众多的争论,其结果使克隆的未来难以预料。

B 课文

克隆动物

自从1996年克隆了多利羊以来,科学家们已经从成熟的细胞中克隆了各种各样的哺乳动物,包括牛、羊、猪、猫和兔子。当科学家们在动物克隆上取得了一些显著的成绩时,困难也依然存在。肉体细胞核的转移是无效的——没有几只克隆胚胎通过出生幸存下来。例如,2001年为了通过实验诞生出第一只克隆兔,科学家移植了371个胚胎到代理母体中,但只产下了6只克隆兔。

也许更为麻烦的是,早期的研究对于通过肉体细胞核转移而克隆出来的动物的健康问题提出了质疑。随着多利羊的长大,科学家报告她过早地患有关节炎,另外实验发现克隆鼠患有更多的疾病,其寿命也只是普通老鼠的一半。

动物克隆可能会有更多的遗留问题。在野外健康生长的动植物种群通过有性繁殖保持着遗传的多样性——不同的结合中具有各种各样的基因。遗传的多样性能够使一个种群更好地抵抗疾病并适应环境的变化。另一方面,大量的克隆动植物可能缺乏遗传差异。全球的农民种植了很多人工栽培的农作物,包括稻谷,这些人工栽培作物比种植在野外的庄稼遗传变异性要少,因此,单一的病毒就能消灭这些作物。同样,如果牛群中每头牛都来自于一个单一的克隆物,仅一种疾病就可能毁掉整个牛群。

　　尽管有这些缺陷,科学家们相信总有一天动物克隆会促进农业和医学的发展,而且还会防止一些濒危动物的灭绝。在农业方面,克隆牛能生产出高产量的肉或奶;制药业已使用克隆动物为人类生产药物。例如,在苏格兰 PPL 治疗机构研制出的羊奶中含有的蛋白质有助于对血友病的治疗。总有一天,制药公司将克隆出很多基因变异的动物,快速、低成本地获取蛋白质用于药品生产。

　　克隆动物还有可能推动实验室里的实验。研究者们能够创造出许多基因相同的动物来降低实验当中物种标本的可变性,从而使科学家们能够更容易地判断疾病。此外,科学家们可以克隆大量的患有人类疾病的动物,比如关节炎,来研究疾病的进展和潜在的治疗。某些克隆动物,比如猪和羊,能存活数年,科学家们有可能利用这些动物判断它们对药物治疗的长期反应。

REVISION I

Key to Test Paper 1

Part I. Listening Comprehension (15%)

Section A. (5%)
1. A 2. C 3. A 4. B 5. D 6. C 7. D 8. B 9. C 10. C

Section B. (5%)
11. B 12. B 13. A 14. C 15. B 16. A 17. B 18. B 19. C 20. A

Section C. (5%)
21. Atomic waste
23. on the ground
25. reach
27. ocean currents
29. might rise
22. a liquid
24. would quickly spread
26. in barrels
28. produces heat
30. might be broken open

Part II. Grammar and Vocabulary (30%)

Section A. *Fill in the blanks with proper prepositions.* (10%)
31. with 32. on 33. in 34. from 35. of
36. at 37. around 38. as 39. into 40. through

Section B. *Write the words in the right column according to the meaning in the left column, using the given letter as a clue.* (10%)
41. confuse 42. escape 43. predict 44. identify 45. release
46. evaluate 47. desire 48. remarkable 49. identical 50. survive

Section C. *Choose the best answer.* (10%)
51. C 52. D 53. D 54. B 55. B 56. A 57. B 58. B 59. D 60. C
61. C 62. B 63. A 64. B 65. B 66. A 67. C 68. B 69. A 70. A

Part III. Reading Comprehension (30%)

71. C 72. D 73. C 74. C 75. B 76. D 77. C 78. C
79. B 80. D 81. C 82. D 83. A 84. A 85. D

Part IV. Translation (10%)

86. 从水库下泄的水流经并转动涡轮,然后带动发电机发电。
87. 联合国秘书长对在工作现场的医务人员的出色工作表示祝贺。
88. 2004年底发布的最新的官方统计数据显示,中国已有84万名艾滋病病毒感染者。
89. 这项研究增加了对人类能否克隆胎儿的关注。
90. 尽管做出了许多努力,却已证实马很难克隆。

Part V. Practical Writing (15%)

POSTER

The Friendship Cup Championship

Under the Auspices of the Students' Union

Exciting Football Final Between 2 Powers!

All teachers and students are welcome to cheer the players.

Place: The stadium

Time: Friday, 4:30 pm. April 22

Teams: Computer Dept. vs. Economic Trade Dept.

                                    The Recreational & Physical Culture Department

                                            of the Students' Union

April 20, 2005

Tape Scripts for Test Paper 1

Part I. Listening Comprehension (15%)

Section A. Directions: *In this section you will hear 10 statements. Each statement will be read only once. Then there will be a pause. During the pause, you must read the four choices marked A, B, C and D, and decide which is closest in meaning to the sentence you have just heard, and then choose the corresponding letter.* (5%)

1. If he had had more film, he could have taken more pictures.
2. She's older than she looks.
3. Jim can't tell a bird from a chicken.
4. She should have listened to her teacher's advice.
5. It's hard to get used to getting up early.
6. You'll have to read the directions a second time.
7. Anna would rather see a film than a play.
8. I can't believe you weren't born in America.
9. Fifteen of the thirty blood tests were all right.
10. From time to time I make long-distance calls.

Section B. Directions: *In this section, you will hear 10 short conversations. At the end of each conversation, a question will be asked about what was said. The conversation and the question will be spoken only one time. After each question, there will be a pause. During the pause, you must read the four choices marked A, B, C and D, and decide which is the best answer, and then choose the corresponding letter.* (5%)

11. W: Oh, Indiana! I'm from Michigan. But I have cousins in Indianapolis. Maybe you know them.
    M: No, I'm from Portersville.
    Q: Where is the man from?
12. M: Hi, are you new in town? Maybe I could show you the way.
    W: That's okay. My sister will pick me up.
    Q: What does the man offer?
13. W: Tommy! I thought you were going to call from the bus station.
    M: Yes, I tried, but nobody was home.
    Q: What did the man do before he saw the woman?
14. W: That's very kind of you. I really appreciate your helping my little brother.
    M: Never mind, I had some time to kill.
    Q: What did the man mean?

15. W: Don't you know that you can't trust strangers? You haven't changed a bit.
    M: Well, he seemed like a respectable guy and I didn't know how to get here.
    Q: What does the woman mean?
16. M: I'd like to cash a check. May I borrow your pen?
    W: Sure. Don't you have an account here?
    Q: Where does the conversation take place?
17. W: We have to hurry. We are supposed to meet Pat at the restaurant at 6:30.
    M: Oh, great! Which restaurant?
    Q: How many people will be there altogether?
18. W: Hi! I hope I haven't kept you waiting long.
    M: Listen, I just got here myself.
    Q: When did the man arrive?
19. W: Do you know how to use chopsticks?
    M: No, but I'm sure I can handle them.
    Q: What do we learn about the man from the conversation?
20. W: Could you help me put away some groceries so I can start dinner?
    M: Yeah, just a minute.
    Q: What is the woman going to do?

Section C. Directions: *In this section you will hear a passage of about 90 words three times. There are about 20 words missing. First, you will hear the whole passage from the beginning to the end just to get a general idea about it. Then, in the second reading, write down the missing words during the pauses. You can check what you have written when the passage is read to you once again without the pauses.* (5%)

> Then how about the earth we live on? **Atomic waste**, which is usually **a liquid**, cannot be poured out **on the ground**. If it were done, the liquid **would quickly spread**, seep into the ground, and **reach** water, plants, animals and people. You may suggest that atomic waste be placed **in barrels** and buried under the ground, where there are no **ocean currents** to affect the barrels. But you must remember that atomic waste is energy and **produces heat**. If it were buried under the ground, the temperature **might rise** very high and the barrels **might be broken open**.

Unit Five

ADVERTISING AND ADVERTISEMENTS

Objective

By the end of this unit, the learners are required to grasp the following:

I. **Key Words and Phrases**
   1. Words:

   consume, consumer, consumption
   attract, attraction, attractive
   special, specialty, specialize
   inform, information, informative
   product, production, productive

   2. Phrases:

   be described as   consist of   fill with   leaf through
   pass on   point out   result from   result in
   take the place of trace back

II. **Language Structure**
   Word Formation

III. **Practice and Improvement**
   Reading Skills: Speed Reading and Cloze Procedure
   Speaking Skills: Going Shopping
   Listening Skills: Sentence Judgment, Dialogues, and Spot Dictation
   Translation Skills: Phrases and Word Formation
   Writing Skills: Sentence Patterns and Advertisements

Word Usage

Reading Selection

Text A

1) **Advertising** is part of our lives.

   advertise *v.* to make something known generally or in public, especially in order to sell it
   做广告,登广告

   e.g. We advertised through the press.
   我们通过报纸宣传。
   We advertised our car in the local newspaper.
   我们在地方报纸上为我们的车做广告。

   advertisement *n.* 广告

   e.g. We are going to place an advertisement in the newspaper.
   我们将在报纸上登广告。

   advertiser *n.* 刊登广告者,广告客户

2) To realize this fact, you have only to **leaf through** a magazine or newspaper or count the radio or television commercials that you may hear in one evening.

   leaf through to quickly turn the pages of a book or a magazine, reading only a little of it
   迅速翻阅

   e.g. The waiting room was full of people leafing through magazines.
   候诊室里坐满了翻阅杂志的人。

3) Advertising is a big business—and to many people, a fascinating business, **filled with** attraction and excitement.

   fill with to make or become full; to use empty space 充满

   e.g. The children's minds are always filled with strange ideas.
   孩子的头脑中总是充满了古怪的想法。
   She seemed to be suddenly filled with energy.
   她似乎一下子精力充沛起来。

4) Advertising is a difficult business of bringing **information** to great number of people.

   inform *v.* to tell someone about particular facts 通知

   e.g. He informed me of your decision.
   他把你的决定告诉了我。

We must keep ourselves well informed.
我们要保持消息灵通。

information   *n.*   facts about a situation, person, event, etc   通知,消息,见闻,信息

e.g.   *He is a man of wide information.*
他是个博学多闻的人。

For further information (= if you want to know more), please contact your local library.
要想了解更多信息,请与地方图书馆联系。

informational   *adj.*   containing information   报告的,情报的

e.g.   *The purpose of this forum is also to further push forward the informational process of education, to promote the educational development during the tenth five-year plan, and to promote the achievement of the goal of reform.*
论坛的目的仍然是进一步推动我国教育的信息化进程,促进我国"十五"期间教育发展和改革目标的全面完成。

informative   *adj.*   providing a lot of useful information   情报的,提供情报的;见闻广博的

e.g.   *It will be most interesting and informative to hear Mr. Smith.*
届时能聆听到史密斯先生演讲,定会是极为有趣和增长见识的。

This is an informative book.
这是一本资料丰富的书。

5) **At the beginning of** the 20th century, advertising **was described as** "salesmanship in print."

at the beginning of   在……开始的时候,在……之初

e.g.   *A war broke out at the beginning of the year.*
那年年初,爆发了一场战争。

Notes on how to use this dictionary can be found at the beginning of the book.
在字典的开头,有本字典用法说明。

be described as   被称为

e.g.   *He was described as being very clever.*
人家说他非常聪明。

Mao Zedong was described as one of the greatest men of our time.
毛泽东被称为当代最伟大的人物之一。

6) If this definition were **expanded** to include radio and television, it would still stand today.

expand   *v.*   to increase in size, number or importance, or to make something increase in this way   扩大,扩展,扩张,扩充

e.g.   *The writer expanded his short novel into a long one.*
那位作者把他的短篇小说扩展为长篇。

Iron expands when it is heated.
铁加热以后会膨胀。

expanse *n.* a large, open area of land, sea or sky 宽阔的区域；宽阔；苍天
e.g. *The moon's flame brightened the vast expanse of grassland.*
月光照亮了广阔的草原。
There is an expanse of land suitable for farming.
这儿有一片宽广的适合于耕种的土地。

expansive *adj.* covering a large area 广阔的，可扩张的
e.g. *Before our eyes was the expansive glittering lake.*
眼前是广阔而闪烁的湖水。
Wine made the guests expansive.
酒让客人们心情舒畅。

7) Because it takes **a great deal of** time, it increases the cost of **product** or service.

a great deal of a large amount; much 大量的
e.g. *They still need a great deal more money to finish the project.*
要完成这个项目，他们仍需大量资金。
The matter caused her a great deal of trouble.
那件事给她带来很多麻烦。

product *n.* something that is made to be sold 产品，产物
e.g. *Coffee is Brazil's main product.*
咖啡是巴西的主要产物。
This is the product of his labor.
这是他劳动的成果。

production *n.* the process of making or growing goods to be sold; the amount of something that is made or grown by a country or a company 制造，生产
e.g. *The factory was built for the production of automobiles.*
生产汽车的工厂建起来了。
The industrial production of that country has fallen steadily this year.
这个国家的工业生产值今年已下降了。

productive *adj.* resulting in or providing a large amount or supply of something 生产的，生产性的，能产的，多产的
e.g. *Un is a productive prefix.*
un 是一个构词力活跃的前缀。
Productive relations should be suitable for conditions of productive forces.
生产关系应该要适合生产力状况。

over-production *n.* 过多生产，生产过剩

8) It can be traced back as far as the public criers of ancient Greece—who, for a fee, **shouted out** messages about their clients' products to one and all.

shout

① *v.* to speak with a very loud voice, often as loud as possible   呼喊,呼叫
② *n.* when you say something very loudly or make a very loud sound with your voice   呼喊,呼叫

e.g. He shouted with pain.
他疼得直叫。
He shouted for help.
他大声呼救。
We heard shouts for help in the distance.
我们听到远处有呼救声。
A shout arose out of the crowd.
人群中发出一阵吼声。

shout out   大声呼喊

e.g. She shouted out in delight.
她高兴得大声喊叫起来。
I can hear you all right; there's no need to shout out.
我能听得清楚,你不必嚷出来。

9) **Besides** advertising his product, he identified his shop with a red striped shield so that customers could find it easily.

besides   *adv. & prep.*   in addition to; also   此外,除……之外

e.g. I don't like this cloth and, besides, it costs too much.
我不喜欢这种布,而且也太贵。
There are many others besides me.
除我以外,还有很多人。
Besides English, he has to study German.
除了英语,他还要学德语。

10) Large factories **took the place of** small workshops...

take the place of   to be used instead of someone or something   取代,代替

e.g. Airplanes cannot completely take the place of trains.
飞机不会完全代替火车。
It would be difficult to find a man to take the place of the present manager.
找一个人来代替现在的经理是不容易的。

Outline:

I. (Para. 1) Introduction

Advertising is part of our lives.

II. (Para. 2–3) General Information about Advertising

1. Advertising is a big business. (Para. 2)
2. The purpose of advertising is to make people respond to an idea. (Para. 3)

III. (Para. 4–8) The History of Advertising

1. It was described as "salesmanship in print" in the early 20th century. (Para. 4)
2. It is very old. (Para. 5)
3. The first printed advertising in English appeared in 1478. (Para. 6–7)
4. The Industrial Revolution brought a new kind of advertising. (Para. 8)

IV. (Para. 9) Conclusion

Advertising has developed into a highly specialized profession.

Text B

1) Modern advertising men try to **justify** what they do by telling us of the advantages of advertising.

justify *v.* to give or to be a good reason for 证明……是正当的

e.g. This does not justify his long absence.
这不能说明他长期缺席是对的。
Nothing can justify such careless mistakes.
如此粗心的错误不可原谅。
How can you justify your rude behavior?
你有什么理由如此无礼？
The prime minister justified the action of the government.
首相证明政府的行动是正当的。

2) In fact, products could often be sold more cheaply if there were not wasteful **competition** between companies.

compete *v.*
① to try to be more successful than someone or something else 竞争
② to take part in a race or competition 比赛

e.g. It's difficult for a small supermarket to compete against/with the big supermarkets.
小超市很难与大型超市展开竞争。
China is competing with other countries for world market.
中国正与其他国家竞争国际市场。

Twenty girls competed in the race.
20 位姑娘参加了赛跑。

competitor *n.* a person, team or company that is competing against others 竞争者

e.g. *The company easily outsells its competitor.*
该公司的销售额轻而易举地超过竞争对手。

They sign a secret deal with their main competitor.
他们和主要竞争者签订了一项秘密交易协议。

competition *n.* 竞争,竞赛

e.g. *There's a lot of competition between computer companies.*
电脑公司间的竞争很激烈。

She's entered a crossword competition.
她参加了猜字比赛。

competitive *adj.* involving competition 竞争的,竞赛的

e.g. *The price is not competitive.*
这价格不能与同业竞争。

3) This results in expansive advertisement, the cost of which is **passed on** to the public.

pass on 传递

e.g. *Through the efforts of the teachers, knowledge is passed on from generation to generation.*
通过教师的努力,知识一代又一代地传了下去。

4) A magazine has **pointed out** that headache pills without a brand name can be sold very cheaply...

point out to tell someone about some information 指出

e.g. *I feel I should point out how dangerous it is.*
我觉得我应该指出其危险性。

Did he point out where you were wrong?
他有没有指出你什么地方错了?

5) Advertising agencies spend a lot of time doing research into ways of **manipulating** us.

manipulate *v.* to control something or someone to your advantage 操纵;使用

e.g. *Do you know how to manipulate a computer?*
你知道如何使用计算机吗?

The company tried to manipulate stock prices.
这家公司试图操纵股票价格。

6) They organized a survey to **find out** what kinds of people drank each type.

find out to get information about something because you want to know more about it 找

出,发现,查明,认识到

    e.g. *We must find out whom they punished.*
    我们必须查明他们处罚了谁。
    They wanted to find out how long their food supplies would hold out.
    他们想搞清楚粮食供应还能维持多久。
    We must find out what the masses think.
    我们应当了解群众是怎样想的。

7) To their surprise, more than three people to one said they **preferred** the light beer...
    prefer   *v.*   to like, choose or want one thing rather than another?   更喜欢,宁愿
    e.g. *Would you prefer tea or coffee?*
    你喝茶还是喝咖啡?
    He always prefers staying at home.
    他一向比较喜欢待在家里。
    He preferred to stay at home rather than go with us.
    他宁愿待在家里,不愿和我们一起去。
    They preferred her not to go with them.
    他们宁愿她不跟他们去。

8) Many advertisers admit that their work **consists** mainly **of** creating imaginary differences between products that are nearly the same.
    consist of   由……组成
    e.g. *A week consists of seven days.*
    一星期由七天组成。
    The team consists of four Europeans and two Americans.
    这个队由四个欧洲人和两个美国人组成。

Outline:

I.   **(Para. 1) Introduction**
    Modern advertising men try to justify what they do.

II.   **(Para. 2–4) The Advantages of Advertising**
    1. It reduces the price of goods. (Para. 2)
    2. It gives information to the customers. (Para. 3)
    3. It improves the quality of goods. (Para. 4)

III.   **(Para. 5–8) The Truth about Advertising**
    1. People very often do not know what they want and why they want it. (Para. 5)
    2. The author shows an example of the psychology of shoppers. (Para. 6–7)

3. Advertising made the public believe that it was important to have new things. (Para. 8)

IV. (Para. 9) Conclusion
Advertising is of great importance in our daily life.

Key to Unit 5

Exercises for Reading Comprehension

I. Answer the following questions.

1. Yes. Advertising is part of our lives. Most people see and hear several hundred advertising massages every day. And people respond to the many devices that advertisers use to gain their attention.
2. Advertising is a big business—and to many people, a fascinating business, filled with attraction and excitement. It is part literature, part art, and part show business.
3. The purpose of advertising is to make people respond—to make them react to an idea, such as helping prevent forest fires, or to make them want to buy a certain product or service.
4. The most effective way to sell something is through person-to-person contact.
5. The cost of person-to-person selling is high, because it takes a great deal of time, and it increases the cost of product or service.
6. Advertising is very old. It can be traced back as far as the public criers of ancient Greece—who, for a fee, shouted out messages about their clients' products to one and all. But it first became important in the late 15th century.
7. Because in the 15th century, the merchants of the rapidly growing cities and towns needed a way to tell people where their goods could be bought.
8. The first printed advertisement in the English language appeared in 1478.
9. The Industrial Revolution, in the 18th and 19th centuries, brought a new kind of advertising. Large factories took the place of small workshops, and goods were produced in large quantities. Manufactures used the newly built railroads to distribute their products over wide areas. They had to find many thousands of customers in order to stay in business. They could not simply tell people where shoes or cloth or tea could be bought—they had to learn how to make people want to buy a specific product. Thus modern advertising was born.
10. Advertising agencies began to develop in the United States just after the Civil War.
11. Because it increases the number that are sold.
12. Products could often be sold more cheaply if there were not wasteful competition between companies.
13. Most advertising does more than inform, and much is misleading.

14. No, it doesn't.
15. Fear, greed, wanting to be better than one's neighbors.
16. The purpose of the advertising agencies is to manipulate the customers.
17. No, they don't.
18. Two other reasons for the sudden interest in psychology were the over-production of many goods, which made companies desperate to sell more, and the fact that brands of many products were becoming more and more alike
19. Through advertising, they made them dissatisfied with an old car or piece of furniture, even when there was nothing wrong with it.
20. Today, many advertisers admit that their work consists mainly of creating imaginary differences between products that are nearly the same.

II. **Find words in the text which mean approximately or the same as the following, using the given letter as a clue.**

1. commercial
2. definition
3. ancient
4. mislead
5. religious
6. justify
7. competition
8. polish
9. greed
10. manipulate

III. **Choose the correct word form to complete each sentence, and make proper changes where necessary.**

1. a. productive   b. productions
2. a. consumed   b. consumption
3. a. informed   b. information
4. a. special   b. specializes
5. a. attraction   b. was attracted

IV. **Complete the sentences with the given expressions, and change the forms where necessary.**

1. be traced back
2. consists of
3. resulted in
4. point out
5. results from
6. filled with
7. was described as
8. take the place of
9. leaf through
10. is passed on

Exercises for Language Structure

I. Look at the words listed below. Write down their negative or opposite forms next to the appropriate prefixes. The first has been done for you.

dis-	disagree	distrust	disloyal	disobey
il-	illegal	illegible	illogical	
im-	impractical	impossible	immature	imperfect	impatient
in-	inconvenient	incapable	inability	insecure	invisible
ir-	irrelevant	irresponsible		
un-	unhappy	unwilling	unofficial	
non-	nonsmoker			

II. Make adjectives from the boxes of suffixes and words to fill in the sentences below according to the sentence meaning.

1. comfortable
2. accessible
3. retired
4. dutiful
5. creative
6. amusing
7. cautionary
8. idiotic
9. selfish
10. effortless
11. orderly
12. foggy

III. From the two boxes below, choose one word from each to form appropriate jointed or hyphened compounds, according to the meaning of the sentence. The first part of each compound word comes from Box A. The first one is done for you.

1. sewing-machine
2. freezing-point
3. seaside
4. good-looking
5. blood-test
6. sunrise
7. food-poisoning
8. dark-room
9. easy-going
10. hardback

IV. Choose a suitable verb from the box below and convert it to a noncount or count to complete the meaning of each sentence.

1. a reason
2. the smell
3. wants
4. the taste
5. respect
6. sense
7. worries
8. doubts
9. think
10. dislikes

V. Find the choice that best completes each of the following sentences.
   1. B   2. B   3. B   4. B   5. B   6. B   7. B   8. B   9. B   10. C

Practice and Improvement

Reading Skills

Speed Reading I
1. B   2. D   3. A   4. C   5. D   6. F   7. F   8. T   9. F   10. T

Speed Reading II
1. C   2. B   3. B   4. D   5. B   6. F   7. F   8. T   9. T   10. F

Cloze Procedure
1. B   2. A   3. B   4. A   5. B   6. C   7. B   8. C   9. B   10. C

Communication Function

Buying a New Mobile Phone

A: Good morning.
B: Good morning. Is this the mobile phone advertised on television?
A: Yes, this is our brand-new phone.
B: Ok. Who's it designed for?
A: It's ideal for business people who are out of the office a lot.
B: Is it easy to carry along?
A: Sure, as you can see, it's very compact; it is easy to carry along in your case, handbag, or pocket.
B: Does it have any network connection?
A: Yes. It can connect with all major international telephone networks.
B: That's very impressive. How much is it?
A: It is 120 dollars, including batteries. It's very affordable, I think.

Listening Comprehension

I. 1. A   2. D   3. C   4. D   5. D   6. A   7. C   8. A   9. C   10. B

II. 1. B   2. D   3. B   4. B   5. C   6. D   7. B   8. A   9. D   10. D

III. 1. for daily life   2. and so on
     3. the trade name   4. market the products

5. the consumers
7. on the market
9. Generally speaking
6. by the price
8. market research
10. to sell well

Translation Skills

I. Translate the following into English.

1. Nowadays, artificial intelligence robots have taken the place of workers in many assembly lines.
2. Advertising distributes the selling message to many people.
3. Does the idea of working for a venture company appeal to you?
4. Cheap used to mean attractive, but this idea is outdated nowadays.
5. Advertising controls the public's spending habits to some extent. One of the bad results is that what many consumers buy is not necessarily what they want.

II. Translate the following into Chinese.

1. 从积极的角度看,广告有助于消费者获得商品信息。但从消极的角度看,广告使消费者购买商品时支付一笔额外的费用。
2. 为争取更大的市场份额,推销自己的产品,各生产厂家均在广告上做了大笔投入。
3. 这种产品之所以受欢迎,是因为它的广告使人们常把它与母爱联系起来。
4. 市场上的商品琳琅满目,消费者有了更广泛的选择。
5. 20世纪40年代以来,美国商人一直借助调查手段来调研、命名、包装和促销产品。

Writing Skills

I. Rewrite each of the sentences after the models.

Model A:

1. One has to pay close attention to English idioms in order to learn the language faster and use it more freely.
2. We must keep our eyes open in order to learn more things around us.
3. The Chinese people are working hard in order to build China into a prosperous country.
4. Marx kept on learning Russian in order to read Russian papers and have a full understanding of the situation in Russia.
5. Edison made thousands of experiments in order to settle the problem.

Model B:

1. Computerized machinery are of great use in modern farming.
2. The document is of great significance in history.
3. Pollution is of great harm to the environment.
4. What the student advisor said is of great value to the freshmen.
5. Internet is of great help to the scholars and the public.

II. Practical Writing

> ### Golden Land Building on a Golden Land Location
> ◆ Located on the bank of Liangma River, Chaoyang District, Beijing
> ◆ Modern integrated commercial and residential complex, comprising office units, apartments and an up-market shopping mall
> ◆ Water, electricity, gas, heat available
> ◆ Mortgage provided by China Investment Bank, Beijing Branch
> ### Visitors are Welcome
> Sales hotline: Tel: (8610) 67140558, 67140559
>
> Sales office: 32 Liangmaqiao Road, Chaoyang District, Beijing
>
> Developer: Beijing Royal Garden Real Estate Development Co. Ltd.

Tape Scripts for Listening Comprehension

I. Directions: *In this section you will hear 10 statements. Each statement will be read only once. Then there will be a pause. During the pause, you must read the four choices marked A, B, C and D, and decide which is closest in meaning to the sentence you have just heard, and then choose the corresponding letter.*

1. Kate has a red and blue pencil.
2. Fasten your seat belt, please.
3. I'd like to drive to the concert but my brother hasn't the car tonight.
4. The red book is 2 dollars and the blue one is a dollar more.
5. No one could enjoy football better than Jack does.
6. It is 8 o'clock now, the concert started 30 minutes ago.
7. Since there aren't any tickets left for the concert, let's go to the movies instead of going home.
8. Jane asked Jim not to speak loudly.
9. The boy would have been killed if the train hadn't stopped quickly.
10. They are looking at the monkeys running around the rocks.

II. Directions: *In this section, you will hear 10 short conversations. At the end of each conversation, a question will be asked about what was said. The conversation and the question will be spoken only once. After each question there will be a pause. During the pause, you must read the four choices marked A, B, C and D, and decide which the best answer is, and then choose the corresponding letter.*

1. W: I tried to solve the problem but it was beyond my understanding.
   M: Oh, why don't you ask me?
   Q: What does the woman mean?

2. W: I'm always nervous when I'm around the teacher.
   M: Me, too. I believe she is too hard to us.
   Q: How do the students think of their teacher?
3. W: What a beautiful rose! Is it for me?
   M: Of course, it is. Don't you remember it's your birthday?
   Q: What did the man do for the woman on her birthday?
4. W: Tell me, John, what do you like to do in your spare time?
   M: Well, I like swimming, reading novels and listening to music.
   Q: What are they talking about?
5. M: Many of my classmates ride bikes to school. I wish I had one, too.
   W: If you had got a perfect mark in maths, I would have bought one for you.
   Q: What can we know about the man?
6. W: What would you do if you had a million U. S. dollars?
   M: I would stop teaching English around the world.
   Q: What is the man?
7. W: Do you do your own laundry?
   M: No, my mother does my shirts; and I take my suits to the cleaner's.
   Q: Who washes the man's shirts?
8. W: Did you catch your train this morning?
   M: If I had got up earlier, I wouldn't have missed it.
   Q: What do we learn about the man?
9. W: Why do all your clothes fit you so well?
   M: I never buy clothes in stores. All my clothes are tailor-made.
   Q: Who made the man's clothes?
10. W: How much did the trousers you're wearing cost?
    M: Well, the material cost me $158.00 and the tailor charged me with $200.58.
    Q: How much all together?

III. Directions: *In this section you will hear a passage of about 90 words three times. There are about 20 words missing. First, you will hear the whole passage from the beginning to the end just to get a general idea about it. Then, in the second reading, write down the missing words during the pauses. You can check what you have written when the passage is read to you once again without the pauses.*

The products **for daily life** are basically the same—cooking oil, soap, household cleaning materials **and so on**. What the consumer has nowadays is the choice of brand—**the trade name** given to the companies that **market the products**. Shops decide which products they think they can sell best to you and me—**the consumers**. We decide which brand of soap to buy. We might be influenced **by the price**, the packaging, or both. When a new product brand is put **on the market**, the promotion campaign is considered to be very important and **market**

research is taken very seriously. **Generally speaking**, the more widespread the promotion (TV, magazines, buses etc.) the more likely the product is **to sell well**.

Online Resources:

1. http://www.fortmorgantimes.com/Stories/0,1413,164~8305~3028425,00.html
2. http://www.adjab.com/2005/08/26/daley-talks-about-the-future-of-advertising/
3. http://www.sbpost.ie/breakingnews/breaking_story.asp?j=81509560&p=8y5x9934&n
4. http://www.prweb.com/releases/2005/8/prwebxml276632.php
5. http://www.internetretailer.com/dailyNews.asp?id=15908

Text Translation for Reference

第五单元 广 告

A 课文

广 告

广告与我们的生活密不可分。要了解这一事实，你只要翻一翻报纸、杂志，或数一数你一个晚上收听到的广播、电视广告数量就行了。绝大多数人每天都会看到和听到数百个广告信息，同时人们对广告商用来吸引他们注意力的许多手段也做出了反应。

广告是一宗大买卖，对许多人而言，它还是极具吸引力的事业，充满着魅力和激情。它既是文学、艺术，又是演艺事业。

广告是一项非常艰难的事业，它要给人们带来信息。广告的目的是让人们对一个想法做出反应，比如有助于防止森林大火，或者让他们想要购买某件商品或接受某项服务。

在20世纪初，广告被称为"印刷品上的推销"，如果这个定义被扩大到包括收音机和电视机，那么到了今天该定义同样成立。销售商品最有效的方法是通过人与人的直接接触，但这种销售方式的成本很高，因为它要花费大量的时间，增加了产品或服务的成本。而广告可以在同一时间将销售信息发送给很多人。

广告的历史久远，它可以追溯到古希腊时期的小商小贩。他们为了酬金，或向一人推销，或当众大声呼喊着有关他们客户商品的信息。但是在15世纪末，快速增长的城镇商人需要有一种方法告诉人们去哪里能购买他们的商品，这时，广告就变得尤为重要了。

第一个印有英文的广告出现于1478年，比莎士比亚的第一部戏剧的诞生还早了一个多世纪。这份最早的广告是英国第一位印刷家——威廉·克莱克斯顿的作品，他曾用广告大肆宣传自己印刷的宗教书籍。克莱克斯顿沿着伦敦的主要街道张贴了一些小张的印刷广告，除了为自己的产品做广告以外，他还给他的商店安装了红条纹盾牌标志，以便顾客们容易找到。

这种简单的信息式的同类型广告仍在使用。比如路边的广告牌就告诉旅客们，他们沿路就可以买到新鲜的玉米或者在下一个镇子就有旅店。

18、19世纪的工业革命带来了一种新型的广告。大工厂取代了小作坊，商品成批量生产，厂商用新建的铁路将产品运送到更远的地方。他们必须得找到千千万万个顾客，以便把生产继续下去。他们不是简单地告诉人们哪里可以买到鞋子、布匹或茶叶，他们必须学会如何让人们想去购买特有的商品。这样人们开始利用广告来开拓新的市场。当人们开始意识到他们有权了解新产品及更好的产品时，现代广告就真正起到了有助于提高人们生活水准的作用。

美国南北战争后，广告代理机构开始在美国兴起。刚开始这些代理商仅仅在不同的媒体，主要是报纸杂志上出售广告篇幅，但是不久他们增加了撰写广告和制作广告的服务。从这以后，广告已经发展成为高度专业化的行业。

B 课文

广告的利与弊

现代广告人努力想通过告诉我们广告的优势以证明他们所做的一切都是非常合理的。

因此，有人说广告因为促使商品销售量的增长而降低了商品的价格。实际上，如果公司间没有资源浪费性的竞争，产品还能卖得更便宜。这种竞争导致了昂贵的广告宣传，这些费用也就分摊到了公众身上。某杂志已经指出，没有商标名称的头痛药卖得非常便宜，但是相同的药，如果广告开销一年为50万英镑，其售价就是原来的五倍。

其二，有人认为广告给顾客带来了信息。当然，广告非常有助于顾客了解当地电影院的放映信息，掌握商品降价日期，甚至某些商品的到货情况。但是大多数广告远远不止提供信息，很多的广告还在误导消费者。你如果相信电视中所播放的所有"测试"都是真实的话，那你就大错特错了。比如在一个上光剂的广告中，为了呈现出有光泽的效果，黑色玻璃代替了木头；另外在一则猫食广告中，使用的是新鲜肉，因为猫拒绝吃罐装食品；在洗衣粉广告中使用的"雪白"的衬衫很可能是淡蓝色的（淡蓝色在彩色电视上呈白色）。

最后，还有人说广告改善了商品的质量，因为广告商担心他们的声誉。在很多情况下，的确如此，但也有人论证说，广告已经让人们心甘情愿地接受质量下乘的商品。把廉价家具店销售的质量下乘的时尚家具赝品和过去为穷人制作的质量上乘的家具进行对照就清楚了。

事实是广告商力图利用的不是人们的美好情感，而是人们内心的恐惧、贪婪以及想胜过别人的虚荣心。广告代理花费大量时间研究如何诱导顾客，而且已证实人们通常并不知道他们想要买什么，甚至即使当他们知道要买什么，他们也不明白自己为什么想要买。难怪广告商对购物者的心理如此感兴趣。

几年前，人们发现调查并不是非常有帮助的。每当采访时，人们总是说他们认为自己喜欢的东西，而不说他们真正喜欢的东西。举个例子，一家公司生产了两种啤酒，一种普通的，另一种是价钱稍贵，度数较低的。他们组织了一次调查想了解哪一类人饮用哪一种啤酒。出乎他们意料的是：几年来，尽管公司销售的普通啤酒一直是另一种啤酒的九倍多，但四分之三以上的人说他们喜欢低度啤酒。人们对公司的问题似乎是这样理解的："你是喝口感好的啤酒，还是只喝普通的啤酒？"

对心理学突然感兴趣的另外两个原因是，一是许多商品的生产过剩，使得公司不顾一切地兜售；二是许多产品的品牌变得越来越相似。

公司认为人们不应该将商品保留过长的时间，这点非常重要。通过广告，公司让顾客不满意自己的旧车或旧家具，即使它们没有任何破损；他们还使公众相信拥有全新的东西是非常重要的。一些公司甚至开始生产一些仅仅只能维持很短一段时间的商品。

如今广告是我们日常生活中很重要的一部分。许多广告商承认他们的工作主要是在几乎相同的产品之间创造想像的差别。举例来说，在眼睛被遮住的情况下，几乎没有烟民能够说出两种不同品牌的香烟之间的差别。可如果你相信广告，你就不会相信这个例子了。

Unit Six

COMPUTERS CONCERNING YOU

Objective

By the end of this unit, the learners are required to grasp the following:

I. **Key Words and Phrases**
   1. Words:

decrease	diagnose	medical	medicine	patient
program	specialist	symptom	treat	treatment

   2. Phrases:

be up to	come up with	keep track of	make a diagnosis of
make house calls	on demand of	refer to	refer... to
step by step	take over		

II. **Language Structure**
   Inversion

III. **Practice and Improvement**
   Reading Skills: Speed Reading and Cloze Procedure
   Speaking Skills: Booking a Transport Ticket
   Listening Skills: Sound Recognition, Dialogues, and Spot Dictation
   Translation Skills: Phrases and Inversion
   Writing Skills: Sentence Patterns and Student's Grade Report

Word Usage

Reading Selection

Text A

1) We've sold a lot of automobiles recently, so I think we ought to **enlarge** our plant.

   enlarge *v.* to become bigger or to make something bigger 扩大,放大

   e.g. They wanted to enlarge the business relationships this year.
   他们今年想扩大业务关系。
   Will this print enlarge well?
   放大这张照片,效果会好吗?

2) Computers can do simple calculations—add, subtract, multiply, and divide—with lightning speed and **perfect** accuracy.

   perfect
   ① *adj.* complete and correct in every way, of the best possible type or without fault 完美的;正确的
   ② *v.* to make something free from faults 使完美,使熟练

   e.g. She speaks perfect English.
   她说一口极好的英语。
   None of us is perfect.
   我们谁也不是完美无缺的。
   It seems to me that you should perfect your plan.
   似乎你还应该完善一下计划。

3) Not only can computers do the four operations very quickly, but also gather **a wide range of** information for many purposes.

   a range of 一系列

   e.g. The encyclopedia provides a wide range of knowledge.
   这本百科全书提供了广博的知识。
   There is a large range of motors for sale.
   有一系列待售的汽车。

4) In business and industry, computers are used to prepare factory inventories, **keep track of** sales trends and production needs, mail dividend checks, and **make out** company payrolls.

   keep track of 记录,掌握……的情况

e.g. *As a doctor, Mr. Stewart has to keep track of the latest developments in medicine.*
作为一名医生，斯图尔特先生必须了解医学的最新发展动态。
The computer can keep track of the patient's progress and sound an alarm in the event of danger.
计算机能掌握病人的病情变化，并在万一发生危险时发出警报。

make out 编制；填写；理解；辨认出

e.g. *She is making out an account.*
她正在作会计账。
The teacher made out the report cards and gave them to the students to take home.
老师开出成绩单交给学生带回家。
Please make out a bill for these goods.
请开一张这些货的发票。
We couldn't make out what she meant.
我们不懂她是什么意思。

5) Some multinational corporations... can provide goods and services **on demand of** the customers through e-commerce, thus greatly reducing the costs and inventories.

on demand of 根据……的需要，按照……的要求

e.g. *Some companies, like Lenovo and TCL in China, provide goods and services on demand of the market and customers.*
有些公司，像中国的联想和TCL，根据市场和顾客的需要提供产品和服务。

6) The future will bring major advances in computer technology and application, which will help man **in his efforts** to improve his world.

in one's efforts 尽力，不遗余力

e.g. *In their efforts to reduce crime the government expanded the police force.*
为了不遗余力地降低犯罪，政府加大了警力。

7) Even though computers **are taking over** some of the tasks that were once done by our own brains...

take over 接管，把……接过来

e.g. *You'd better consult with your parents before you take over your brother's job.*
在你接替你兄弟的工作之前，你最好与你的父母商量一下。
We now living in a world in which robots take over much of the work.
在我们这个时代，机器人承担了大量的工作。

Outline:

I. (Para. 1–3) Introduction

Suppose a situation that you need a computer.

II. (Para. 4–9) Functions of Computers

1. Computers can do simple calculations with lightning speed and perfect accuracy. (Para. 4)
2. Computers gather a wide range of information for many purposes. (Para. 5)
3. They can do many things in business and industry. (Para. 6)
4. They can also store facts and pour them out whenever they are needed. (Para. 7)
5. People come to know the importance of computers. (Para. 8)
6. Adults and children are being taught through distance education. (Para. 9)

III. (Para. 10–11) Conclusion

Computers will not replace us —at least not yet.

Text B

1) Computers can store **all sorts of** data on medical care.

   all sorts of   各种各样的

   e.g. *We saw all sorts (= many types) of animals in the park.*
   在公园我们看到了各种各样的动物。

   There are all sorts of goods in the supermarket during the Spring Festival.
   春节期间,这家超市备有各种各样的商品。

2) Trust it to **make a close examination of** you through all of its stored data?

   make an examination of   对……进行检查

   e.g. *You must make a critical examination of your bad behavior.*
   你必须认真检讨你的不良行为。

   Before entering, Jeff made an examination of the door.
   杰夫进去之前,检查了一下门。

3) Trust it to **come up with** exactly what's causing—and how to **treat** your illness?

   come up with   赶上;提供;补充

   e.g. *We are making our efforts to come up with advanced level.*
   我们正在努力赶上先进水平。

   People can put ideas together in many ways and can come up with new ideas.
   人们可以集思广议,并提出新想法。

   treat   *n.*   to behave towards someone or deal with something in a particular way   对待;处理;治疗;款待

e.g. We should treat animals kindly.
我们应该爱护动物。

We treated him as a friend.
我们对他以朋友相待。

Which doctor is treating you for this trouble?
哪位医生给你治病？

He treated his friends to some beer.
他请朋友喝了些啤酒。

4) Often does one doctor **refer** you **to** another doctor—one who is a specialist in only one area of medicine.

refer... to... to direct someone or something to a different place or person for information, help or action 把……推荐到，将……提交给

e.g. The shop referred the complaint to the manufacturer.
商店把投诉转交给制造商。

We refer the question to them.
我们把这个问题提交他们处理。

You may refer the matter to him if necessary.
必要的话你可以把这件事委托给他。

refer to 参考，咨询，查阅；涉及

e.g. You can't refer to your book when you are in the exam.
考试时不能查阅书。

He referred to me for information.
他向我打听消息。

You can refer to your notes when you are speaking.
你发言时可以看稿子。

5) New **treatments**, new medicine, and new techniques for **diagnosing** illness are being developed all the time.

treat *v.* to use drugs, exercises, etc. to cure a person of a disease or heal an injury 治疗

e.g. The doctor treated his fever with pills.
医生用药片给他退烧。

treatment *n.* 治疗

e.g. Perhaps it's time to try a new course of treatment.
或许该尝试一下新的治疗方法。

treatable *adj.* 能治疗的

e.g. Don't worry. This is a treatable disorder.
别担心，这疾病是可以医治的。

diagnose *v.* to recognize and name the exact character of a disease or a problem, by making an examination 诊断

e.g. *The doctor diagnosed the illness as influenza.*
医生诊断此病为流行感冒。
The teacher diagnosed the boy's reading difficulties.
老师找出那孩子阅读上困难的原因。

diagnosis *n.* a judgment about what a particular illness or problem is, after making an examination 诊断，判断（复数：diagnoses）

e.g. *The doctor has made an initial diagnosis, but there'll be an additional examination by a specialist.*
这医生已做了初步诊断，但还需专家做进一步检查。
The engineer made a complete diagnosis of the bridge's collapse.
工程师对桥的倒塌做了一次彻底的调查分析。

6) Then **it's up to** the doctor to decide which treatment is really the best.
be up to be the responsibility of someone 该由……，轮到……

e.g. *It's up to the manager to make the final decision.*
该由经理作最后的决定。

7) These instructions are "learned" and carried out **step by step.**
step by step dealing with one thing and then another thing in a fixed order 逐步地

e.g. *A foreign language cannot be learned rapidly; it must be learned step by step.*
学外语不能急，只能按部就班地学。
Don't worry—I'll go through the procedure with you step by step.
别担心，我会和你一起逐步完成这项程序。

Outline:

I. (Para. 1–3) Introduction

Would you turn to a computer for help—if you were running a fever?

II. (Para. 4–6) The Difference between the Doctors in the Past and the Doctors of Today

1. A family doctor would come miles to your house if you were ill. (Para. 4)

2. It's not easy to find a doctor who makes house calls, and the reason why. (Para. 5–6)

III. (Para. 7–11) The Difference between Computers and Doctors

1. They can store huge amounts of data without any trouble. (Para. 7)

2. Their memory system can "learn" and "memorize" the latest medical researches and discoveries. (Para. 8)

3. It's up to the doctor to decide which treatment is really the best when PROMIS shows the various treatments it has in its memory. (Para. 9)

4. Some computers have been programmed to be "medical specialists." (Para. 10–11)

IV. (Para. 12) Conclusion
The application of computers is very important in medicine.

Key to Unit 6

Exercises for Reading Comprehension

I. Answer the following questions.

1. Because of its memory and speed, a computer can consider more factors than a human being.
2. I would solve the problems with the aid of a computer because there is a limit to the number of questions the human mind can think about.
3. People began to use computers in 1944.
4. In business and industry, computers are used to prepare factory inventories, keep track of sales trends and production needs, mail dividend checks, and make out company payrolls. It can also keep bank accounts up to date and make out electronic bills.
5. If I'm planning a trip by plane, the computer will find out what route to take and what seat is available, and then book the ticket for me.
6. No, they can't. Only through special training are people able to make effective use of computers.
7. Yes, they can. For example, in Open University of Great Britain, more than 100 thousand students receive distance education, and in China Central Radio & TV University, over one million students take their courses through the Internet or via other media.
8. In some countries, company employees renew their knowledge by on-line learning.
9. The major advances in computer technology and application will help man in his efforts to improve his world.
10. Human brains are more complicated than computers.
11. Yes, they can.
12. No, he can't.
13. At that time, a family doctor would come miles to the house if somebody was ill.
14. Most of us have to travel to a doctor's office if we are ill.
15. No, he doesn't. Often does one doctor refer you to another doctor—one who is a specialist in only one area of medicine because new treatments, new medicines, and new techniques for diagnosing illness are being developed all the time.
16. PROMIS can store the medical records of every patient in the hospital—each patient's chief complaints, general physical descriptions, symptoms, and lab-test results. If the hospital's doctors and nurses want to know the condition of an individual patient, they just feed

instructions into PROMIS and out come the patient's data. PROMIS also works with the doctors as they make their diagnosis of the disease of the patients.

17. No, it isn't. PROMIS can help a doctor choose the most promising treatment for a patient. Then, it's up to the doctor to decide which treatment is really the best.
18. A computer can run by itself for hours on days.
19. No, it can't.
20. Yes, I will. Because I think with the help of computers, a doctor can recommend a treatment that gives his patient the best chance to live a longer, more active life.

II. Find the meanings of the words or expressions in Column (A) from those in Column (B).
1. G   2. B   3. F   4. A   5. I   6. H   7. J   8. D   9. C   10. E

III. Complete the sentences with the given expressions, and change the forms where necessary.
1. makes house calls
2. step by step
3. keep track of
4. have taken over
5. on demand of
6. make a diagnosis of
7. come up with
8. is up to
9. refer... to
10. refers to

IV. Complete the following passage by using appropriate words listed below, and be sure to use appropriate verb forms and appropriate singular or plural forms for nouns.
1. specialist
2. diagnose
3. program
4. patient
5. medical
6. to treat
7. symptoms
8. decrease
9. treatment
10. medicines

Exercises for Language Structure

I. Put the following sentences into the inverted order so as to make the words or phrases underlined more emphatic.
1. Here is your letter.
2. Up goes the production.
3. Little does he know on how to operate the computer.
4. Only in this way can you hope to improve the situation.
5. In came the president and the meeting began.
6. Hardly had we reached the railway station when the train left.
7. Not only was Marx a revolutionary but also as economist.

8. Not until he finished his homework did he go to bed.
9. Nearby is a big orchard.
10. Along the river bank stood a lot of magnificent buildings.

II. **Rewrite the following sentences by using "so", "nor", or "neither" at the beginning of the sentences.**
1. Coal, oil and natural gas are energy resources. So are wood, water power and wind power.
2. A calculator can't think by itself. Nor can a computer.
3. Mr. Kent made a big profit last year. So did Mr. Wood.
4. An ordinary doctor isn't able to diagnose the illness. Neither is a specialist.
5. New treatments are being developed all the time, and so are new medicines.
6. Computer will not replace human brains, and nor will other machines.
7. Computer science will help us to make effective use of computers, and so will computer techniques.
8. TV programs are not interesting this evening, and neither are radio programs.
9. A manufacturer often has to make decisions by himself; so does a manager.
10. I have not made the computer program; nor has she.

III. **Choose the best answer.**
1. A   2. D   3. B   4. C   5. B   6. B   7. D   8. D   9. C   10. B

IV. **Find out which of the underlined parts in each sentence is not correct in written English.**
1. C. when 改为 than
2. A. Weren't we 改为 Were we not
3. A. the world has 改为 has the world
4. D. hadn't he 改为 wouldn't he
5. D. shouldn't we 改为 should we
6. A. we expected 改为 did we expect
7. C. they were 改为 were they
8. A. the missile went 改为 went the missile
9. D. flew it 改为 it flew
10. C. they should 改为 should they

Practice and Improvement

Reading Skills

Speed Reading I
1. D   2. B   3. C   4. D   5. B   6. F   7. F   8. T   9. T   10. F

Speed Reading II
1. B   2. D   3. D   4. C   5. D   6. T   7. T   8. T   9. F   10. T

Cloze Procedure

1. B 2. A 3. B 4. D 5. C 6. B 7. C 8. C 9. D 10. D

Communication Function

II. Conversation

Booking a Railway Ticket for Beijing

A: Can I help you?

B: Yes, I'd like to make a reservation. Do you have any train for Beijing on May 1?

A: Let me check the computer. Yes, there are still some tickets available.

B: Could you tell me about it?

A: Sure. It's Train No. 12, which leaves here at 3:30 p.m. and arrives at Beijing at 9:10 a.m. tomorrow.

B: Is that a short for Beijing?

A: Yes, it is.

B: That's OK. Are there still any sleeping births available on that train?

A: Yes, there are. Will you tell me your name, please?

B: John Smith.

A: Mr. Smith, which do you prefer, hard sleeper or soft sleeper?

B: Soft sleeper, I think. How much is it?

A: That'll be CNY720.

B: It's quite expensive, isn't it? Do you have any discount?

A: I'm afraid not. It's the holiday season, the peak tourism period, you know.

B: I see.

A: Let me check with you again. Train No.12 for Beijing, May 1, soft sleeper. Mr. Smith, is that right?

B: That's right, thank you, Madam.

A: Welcome to take our train, Mr. Smith.

Listening Comprehension

I. 1. B 2. B 3. A 4. B 5. B 6. B 7. B 8. A 9. A 10. A

II. 1. B 2. A 3. B 4. B 5. D 6. B 7. B 8. A 9. D 10. B

III. 1. Unlike   2. electronic
3. on small currents   4. a computer
5. A normal calculator   6. in a minute
7. 1, 400 billion   8. in a second

9. carry
10. all his life

Translation Skills

I. Translate the following into English.

1. Computers can collect a wide range of information for many purposes.
2. Just now he made out a check for USD1,500.
3. Jack is ready to take over his father's business because of his senior age.
4. It's up to Dr. Martin to give us a talk on information technology and application.
5. We can expect that Mr. Green will come up with some useful advice.

II. Translate the following into Chinese.

1. 医用计算机不仅能诊断疾病,而且能照顾病人。
2. 计算机不能代替人脑,其他机器也不能代替人脑。
3. 无线电节目可以用计算机制作。电视节目也可用计算机制作。
4. 昨天夜晚当我们走近汤姆家时,从门前呼地跑出一条大狗。
5. 地震发生之后,接着又是暴风雨,又是下冰雹。

Writing Skills

I. Rewrite each of the sentences after the models.

Model A:
1. Were you a manufacturer, you would like to keep track of sales trends and production needs.
2. Had I been good at mathematics, I would have worked out the difficult problem.
3. Were I ill now, I might turn to PROMIS for help.
4. Should human beings be cloned, it would bring great trouble to the society.
5. Had she been trained, Mary would have operated the computer more effectively.

Model B:
1. Hardly had the instructions been fed in when the computer printed out the answer.
2. No sooner had the suspected SARS patient been found than he was sent to hospital and kept in quarantine.
3. Hardly had he got the factory when the importer gave the manufacturer his order for the goods.
4. No sooner had he arrived at the airport than the plane took off.
5. Hardly had it happened when the computer gathered all the information about it.

II. Practical Writing

   Write a Student's Grade Report according to the given Chinese materials. You can model your writing on the above Student's Grade Report.

用计算机打印一份成绩通知单并填写上你自己的成绩。

Student's Grade Report				
Name:	Class:	No.	Date of birth:	Sex:
Home address:				
Department:	Major:		Length of program:	

Course	2003/2004 Academic year	
	First term	Second term
	Grade	Grade

Tape Scripts for Listening Comprehension

I. **Directions:** *Listen to the following sentences. Choose which word the speaker or the tape says. Tick the right word.*

1. You are trying to decide **whether** or not to build a large factory or to buy more machines.
2. Millions of emails are sent to each other through internet every day, and the **whole** globe turns into a small village owing to computers.
3. The future will bring major advances in computer technology and application, which will help **man** in his efforts to improve his world.
4. Computers can also keep bank accounts up to **date** and make out electronic bills.
5. How do you get **along** with your computer science?
6. The early computers had moving parts made of **metal** and were operated by hand.

7. The first modern computer was **built** at Harvard University in 1944.
8. Computerized shopping, like computerized banking, will be quick, **safe** and convenient.
9. For example, Galaxy III super computer **made** in China can perform 13 billion calculations per second.
10. Are there still any **seats** available on that flight?

II. Directions: *In this section, you will hear 10 short conversations. At the end of each conversation, a question will be asked about what was said. The conversation and the question will be spoken only one time. After each question, there will be a pause. During the pause, you must read the four choices marked A, B, C and D, and decide which the best answer is, and then choose the corresponding letter.*

1. W: We are having a party tonight and it would be inconvenient for you to be here.
   M: Okay, I get the picture.
   Q: What did the man mean?
2. W: This menu is huge. I'm starving. What looks good to you?
   M: Don't bother. Everything sounds good to me.
   Q: Where does the conversation take place?
3. W: Well, Pat studies engineering at night, works as a mechanic during the day and goes skydiving on weekends.
   M: Gosh! That sounds like a lot of work.
   Q: What doe Pat do on weekends?
4. M: Jane, what should I do if I want to get a job?
   W: How about the classified ads?
   Q: What does the woman suggest the man doing?
5. W: Yes? Can I help you?
   M: Yes. Do you still have that apartment for rent?
   Q: What's the probable relationship between the two?
6. M: Hey, I've just got an apartment. Would you like to see it?
   W: I'd love to, but I'm right in the middle of work right now.
   Q: What is her attitude?
7. M: Oh, what's wrong?
   W: I've just got laid off from work. I've got to find another job right away.
   Q: What happened to the women?
8. W: Oh, officer, it's his fault. I've done absolutely nothing wrong.
   M: Right! Relax, and let me see your driver's license.
   Q: What happened?
9. M: Miss Jenny, can you tell me when I can leave the hospital?
   W: I can't make any promises, but you should be working in no time.
   Q: What does the nurse mean?

10. W: I'm afraid I've caught a bad cold and run a high fever.
    M: Take a seat, and let me take your temperature.
    Q: What's the relationship between the two speakers?

III. **Directions:** *In this section you will hear a passage of about 90 words three times. There are about 20 words missing. First, you will hear the whole passage from the beginning to the end just to get a general idea about it. Then, in the second reading, write down the missing words during the pauses. You can check what you have written when the passage is read to you once again without the pauses.*

Unlike simple calculating machines, computers are **electronic**. They have few, if any, moving parts. Computers work **on small currents** of electricity. Electricity flows at a very high speed, and so **a computer** can work very fast. **A normal calculator** can calculate 100 times **in a minute** whereas the most powerful computer can calculate **1,400 billion** times, not in a minute but **in a second**. Such a machine can **carry** out more operations in a few seconds than a good mathematician could do **all his life**.

Online Resources:

1. http://biz.yahoo.com/iw/050824/093855.html
2. http://www.commsdesign.com/news/insights/showArticle.jhtml?articleID=170100315
3. http://www.businesstimes.com.mt/2005/08/24/tech2.html
4. http://www.internetnews.com/ent-news/article.php/3528641
5. http://www.ssc.net.cn/english/kepu2.htm

Text Translation for Reference

第六单元　与你密切相关的计算机

A 课文

计算机：能够思考的机器

假设你是一个汽车制造商，你正考虑是否建造一个大型工厂，或购买更多的机器。你会对自己说："生意一直很好，最近我们已经卖出了很多汽车，所以我认为我们应该扩大我们的厂房。"

或许你会考虑下面的问题：扩大厂房要花费多少钱呢？买车人的数量会增长还是会减少呢？类似这样的问题都需要回答，但是人类所想到的问题总是有限度的。

如果你是处于这种情况，就需要一台计算机了。由于它的存储功能和速度，一台计算机能考虑的因素比人类多多了。尽管人类1944年才开始使用计算机,但是计算机已改变了数百万人的生活。

　　计算机能快速而准确地进行简单的加减乘除四则运算。它们可以在千分之一秒的时间内把两个十位数相乘,而一个普通人笔算这道题,则要花五分钟的时间。举例来说,中国诞生的银河三号巨型计算机能进行每秒130亿次计算,世界上功能最强的计算机能进行每秒14000亿次运算,有了这样的速度,这些计算机可被用于云图的分析、计算人造卫星的轨道等等。

　　计算机不仅能快速地做四则运算,而且能有目的地收集广泛的信息。随着信息技术和网络技术的发展,计算机能彼此连接,顺畅地交流。有了计算机,你能收集任何所需信息,还能联络到远方的人们。数以百万计的电子邮件每天通过互联网相互发送。由于有了计算机,整个地球变成了一个小村庄。

　　在商业和工业中,计算机被用来列出工厂存货清单,掌握销售动向和生产需要,邮寄股息支票,并编制公司的工资表。它还能保存最新的银行账目,编制电子账单。举例来说,它能告诉你在某个超级市场中,哪种牌子的商品最受欢迎。因此,人们能在家通过互联网进行网上购物。某些跨国公司,如美国的IBM公司和微软公司通过电子商务根据顾客的需要来提供产品和服务,因而大大减少了成本和库存。

　　计算机还能存储资料,而且可以随时提取。举例来说,计算机能告诉你明天的天气如何。如果你计划乘飞机旅行,计算机会提示你可乘坐哪个航班,哪个座位,然后帮你订票。

　　世界上所有的发达国家都有计算机,部分发展中国家也是如此。人们逐渐认识到计算机将在他们的国民经济发展中发挥重要的作用。

　　人们只有通过专门的培训才能有效地使用计算机。然而,很多没有经过专门培训的人在日常生活中也能使用计算机。在某些国家,公司职员通过网络学习以更新他们的知识。成年人和孩子们通过远程教育进行学习。举例来说,在英国的开放大学,超过10万的学生接受了远程教育。在中国中央广播电视大学,超过100万的学生通过互联网或者其他媒体进行学习。

　　在商业、工业、科学和教育方面,计算机几乎在每个领域都发挥着越来越重要的作用。未来在计算机技术和应用上所带来的更大进展,将有助于人类改善整个世界。

　　尽管计算机接管了一些人类大脑曾经担任的工作,但是计算机代替不了人——至少目前还不能。我们的大脑比计算机要复杂得多。怎样使用大脑是由人决定,而不是由计算机来决定的。

B 课文

你好,我是计算机医生

　　如果你正在发烧,你会求助于一台计算机吗?

　　计算机在医学治疗上能存储各种类型的数据。但是你会相信一台机器吗?你会信任计算机通过其储存的所有资料对你进行一次仔细的体格检查吗?相信它能准确提供的病因,以及治疗你疾病的办法吗?难道一位医生不比任何机器对你以及你所感觉的情况了解得更多吗?

　　或者换言之怎么样?医学研究上所有最新的发展,以及你身体中正在进行的所有变化,这些对一位医生来说,要掌握的信息是不是太多了?

你可能会听到你的父母在谈论着"过去的美好时光"。那时,如果有人病了,巡诊医生会走上几英里的路来到你家,人们相信那种医生能够了解病人的一切。

　　可如今,能找到一位能家访的医生实属不易。我们中的大多数人不得不来到医生的诊所,而且还不是同一个医生给你看病,经常是一个医生把你推荐给另一个医生——一位仅精通医学某一领域的专家。

　　每年都有越来越多的知识需要医生学习。新的治疗方法、新的药品和新的诊断技术也一直在不断地更新。医生不可能掌握医学每个领域所发生的最新发展情况,他也不可能记住如何利用所有这些最新的发展。

　　但是,计算机会怎么样呢?它们能毫不费力地存储大量的数据。病人所需的特殊信息只需通过按键便能找到。这样就开始了医院里的一场计算机革命。医院专用的一个计算机系统叫做PROMIS(即医用咨询信息系统)。这个咨询信息系统可以储存该医院每个病人的医疗记录——每个病人所陈述的病情、总的身体状况、症状和化验结果。如果这个医院的医生和护士想要知道某个病人的情况,他们只需向该系统输入指令,病人的数据就出来了。当医生为病人做诊断时,医用咨询信息系统也能与他们一起合作。

　　计算机的存储系统能够"获知"和"记住"最新的医学研究和发现,这和存储单个病人的数据一样简单。而且,医用咨询信息系统还可以帮助医生为病人选择最有效的治疗方案。

　　以下便是操作程序。医用咨询信息系统一诊断出病情,就向医生显示其存储器中储存的各种治疗方法。计算机还能存储有关信息,如该治疗方法对医生正在检查的那种类型的病人可能会有怎样的作用,以及治疗会导致什么样的副作用。然后,由医生负责决定哪一种治疗方法最佳。

　　其他的计算机实际上是建议医生如何治疗患有某种疾病的病人。一台计算机能自动运转好几个小时或好几天。输入计算机的一系列的指令,称为程序。计算机接受这些指令并逐步执行。计算机完成了程序之后,就会自动地把解决办法打印出来。当然,没有被编进程序的疾病治疗方法,计算机是不能进行诊断或提出建议的。

　　某些计算机已经通过编程而成为"医学专家"了,也就是说,一台计算机可以治疗患有某种疾病的病人了。

　　在医学上计算机的应用是非常重要的。有了计算机的帮助,医生能够给他的病人推荐最佳治疗方案,让病人更长寿、更积极地生活。

Unit Seven

THE INTERNET CONCERNING YOU

Objective

By the end of this unit, the learners are required to grasp the following:

I. Key Words and Phrases

1. Words:

   complain, complaint   digit, digital   download, upload
   society, social   surf, surfer

2. Phrases:

   access to   be engaged in   be inferior to   open... to
   click onto the net keep up with   log onto
   on the other hand stop by   to one's astonishment

II. Language Structure

Preposition

III. Practice and Improvement

Reading Skills: Speed Reading and Cloze Procedure
Speaking Skills: Having an Interview
Listening Skills: Sentence Judgment, Dialogues, and Spot Dictation
Translation Skills: Phrases and Prepositions
Writing Skills: Sentence Patterns and Resumes

Word Usage

Reading Selection

Text A

1) Now many American high schools **are opening** these computer centers to their students.
   open... to   available; not limited   对……开放,公开,开放
   e.g.   The competition is open to anyone over the age of sixteen.
   16 岁以上的人都可参加这个比赛。
   Is the library open to the general public?
   图书馆对普通公众开放吗?

2) The Cyber Café now has sixteen computers, a printer and a device called a **scanner**.
   scan   *v.*   to look at something carefully, with the eyes or with a machine, in order to obtain information   扫描,浏览
   e.g.   He scanned the newspaper while having his breakfast.
   他在吃早饭的时候浏览了一下报纸。
   The compiler scanned the source code.
   编译程序对源程序代码进行了一次扫描。
   scanner   *n.*   a device for making images of the inside of the body or for reading information into a computer system   扫描仪
   e.g.   These electric engineers are working on a new type of photo electric scanner.
   这些电器工程师正在努力研制一种新型的光电扫描器。

3) School official Ann Hengerer says students use the Internet to **acquire** information they need.
   acquire   *v.*   to obtain something   获得,学到
   e.g.   We ought to acquire these excellent qualities.
   我们应当学到这些优良品质。
   He had acquired information concerning Mr. Tom from the lawyer.
   他从律师那儿获得了有关汤姆先生的消息。

4) They also **upload** their electronic teaching plans and course wares **onto** the school website for the students to review their lessons after class.
   upload... onto   to copy or move programs or information to a larger computer system or to the Internet   往……上载
   download... from   to copy or move programs or information into a computer's memory, especially from the Internet or a larger computer   从……下载

e.g. *It also provides information about where to download Microsoft's new web browser, Internet Explorer.*
它也提供一些关于在哪儿下载微软的新浏览器 Internet Explorer 的信息。
They are downloading cargo from a transport aircraft.
他们正在从运输飞机卸下货物。

5) The Cyber Café also serves a social purpose, and visitors can **stop by** for a drink of coffee, tea or hot chocolate.

stop by 逗留,停留,顺便拜访

e.g. *The bus stopped by the tree.*
公共汽车停在那棵树旁。
I'll stop by on my way home.
我将在回家的路上顺便进去看看。

Summary:

It is reported that cyber cafés have been established in many high schools of the United States. Officials of B-CC High School say a cyber café helps students who have no computer or cannot use the Internet at home.

The idea for a cyber café at B-CC High School began three years ago, and many supported the idea. Now, the students use the Internet to acquire information they need, send and receive emails. And they also write homework and require papers on the computers. Teachers can also make their teaching researches and guide the students how to make use of the learning sources on the Internet.

The cyber café also serves a social purpose.

Text B

1) She was sitting in her own living room in Beijing chatting **face to face** with her brother thousands kilometers away at the Spring Festival.

face to face　meeting someone directly in the same place　面对面

e.g. *He had a face-to-face conference with his opposite number at the American Embassy.*
他在美国大使馆与他的对手举行了面对面的会谈。
The burglar turned the corner and found himself face to face with a policeman.
那窃贼转过墙角,迎面碰上一个警察。
They've often talked to each other on the telephone, but they've never met each other face to face.
他们常常互相通电话,但从来没有见过面。

2) Like Deng and her brother, an increasing number of the senior Chinese **are surfing** the Internet nowadays.

surf *v.*

① to ride on a wave as it comes towards land, while standing or lying on a special board   在激浪上驾(船),在……冲浪

② to spend time visiting a lot of websites   浏览各种网站

e.g. Many towns and cities have cyber cafes where you can surf the Internet/Net/Web.
城里都有许多网吧,你可在网上浏览各种网站。
They go surfing every weekend.
他们每个周末都去冲浪。

surfer *n.*   a person who rides on a wave on a special board   冲浪运动员;网虫

3) A few months ago, at her brother's urging, Deng installed a **digital** camera on her computer and started to **engage in** Yahoo chat.

digit *n.*   any one of the ten numbers 0 to 9   数字

e.g. The number 410 contains three digits.
数字 410 中包括三个数目字。

digital *adj.*   describing information, music, an image, etc. that is recorded or broadcast using computer technology   数字的,数码的

e.g. It's a digital camera /digital TV.
这是部数码相机/数字电视机。

be engaged (in)   be busy with; work at   忙于,从事

e.g. He is engaged in making preparations for the conference on educational work.
他正忙于筹备教育工作会议。

engage in   to take part in something   使从事于,参加

e.g. The two governments have agreed to engage in a comprehensive dialogue to resolve the problem.
这两个政府同意参加全面对话以解决这一问题。

4) **To my astonishment**, he still looked pretty healthy.

to one's astonishment   to one's great surprise   令人惊讶的是

e.g. To the astonishment of her colleagues, she resigned.
令她同事惊讶的是她辞职了。

5) Deng has learned a lot about the computer from her brother, who **logs** onto the Internet every morning after breakfast.

log

① *n.*   a thick piece of tree trunk or branch   原木,圆木,木材

② *v.*   to cut down trees so that you can use their wood   伐木

③ *v.*   to officially record something   把……记入

e.g. The forest has been so heavily logged that it is in danger of disappearing.

这片森林遭到了严重的砍伐,以致濒临荒芜。

He logged the ship's speed at 10 knots.

他在航海日记上记下船速每小时10海里。

They asked the pilot how many hours he had logged.

他们问那飞行员累积了多少飞行时数。

6) Dr. Deng is especially pleased that the Internet has enabled him to **keep up with** the latest development in medicine.

keep up with 跟上,保持

e.g. Don't run—I can't keep up with you.

别跑了,我赶不上你了。

Are wages keeping up with inflation?

工资跟得上通货膨胀吗?

7) It used to be that we doctors in the western hinterlands felt **inferior to** our counterparts in coastal areas...

inferior *adj.* not good, or not as good as someone or something else 差的,次的

inferior to 在……之下,次于,不如

e.g. It is inferior in quality.

这东西质量低劣。

He is inferior to others in many respects.

他在许多方面不如别人。

Anna's work is so good that the other children feel inferior to her.

安娜的作业做得太好了,别的孩子都感到不如她。

8) "But now there are many special medical websites that have bridged the gap, giving us **access to** the latest information in our fields," Dr. Deng said.

access *n.* the method or possibility of approaching a place or person, or the right to use or look at something 通道;访问

e.g. There is no access to the street through that door.

穿过那个门没有通向大街的路。

The only access to that ancient castle is along a muddy track.

去那座古老城堡的惟一通道是一条泥泞小路。

9) "Retired life doesn't **depress** me at all, because the Internet has made it possible for me to maintain ties with the world around," she said.

depress *v.*

① to cause someone to feel unhappy and without hope for the future 使沮丧,使消沉

② to reduce the value of something, especially money 降低

e.g. The rainy days always *depress* me.
雨天总是使我沮丧。
He was depressed because he had not passed his examinations.
他很沮丧，因为他没有通过考试。
Does mass unemployment depress wages?
大量人口失业会使工资降低吗？
They feared that rising inflation would further depress the economy.
他们担心不断上升的通货膨胀会进一步削弱经济。

10) "If I were only to teach my students the old skills and knowledge that I acquired decades ago, they would **complain**," he said.

complain   *v.*   to say that something is wrong or not satisfactory   抱怨

e.g. They complained about the food.
他们抱怨这糟糕的食物。
Almost immediately he began to complain about the weather.
他几乎马上就开始抱怨起天气来了。
Joan is always complaining about something.
琼总是满腹牢骚。

complaint   *n.*   when someone says that something is wrong or not satisfactory   抱怨，牢骚

e.g. If your neighbors are too noisy then you have cause for complaint.
如果你的邻居太喧哗，你就有理由投诉。
He didn't like the meal so he made a complaint to the manager of the restaurant.
他不喜欢这顿饭，所以他向餐馆经理抱怨了一通。

Summary:

Internet is becoming more and more important to both the young and the elderly netizens. An increasing number of senior Chinese are surfing the Internet nowadays.

The text tells us a vivid story about two senior surfers. They are siblings, and live in different cities, far away from each other. The sister, a retired newspaper editor in her late 70s, can sit in her own living room chatting face to face with her brother, a retired specialist in blood disease. Checking and sending emails has become an indispensable part of the sister's life, while the brother said it's necessary for him to refresh his knowledge through the Internet, and the Internet is also a part of his life and work.

Key to Unit 7

Exercises for Reading Comprehension

I. Answer the following questions.

1. Cyber cafés have been established in many high schools of the United States.
2. They are computer centers in which computers are connected to the Internet.
3. Thirteen percent of the students at the school are from poor families.
4. No, they didn't.
5. Officials in the area supported the idea, and so did an organization called the Bethesda-Chevy Chase High School Educational Foundation.
6. The B-CC High School Educational Foundation includes parents, teachers, former students, and business, community and other leaders.
7. The foundation collected more than one hundred and seventy thousand dollars for the cyber café.
8. The cyber café now has sixteen computers, a printer and a device called a scanner.
9. The students can use the Internet to acquire information they need. They also write homework and required papers on the computers. In addition, they can send and receive e-mails.
10. The teachers can make their teaching researches and guide the students how to make use of the learning sources on the Internet. They also upload their electronic teaching plans and course wares onto the school website for the students to review their lessons after class.
11. Because of the development of information technology and application, Internet is becoming more and more important to both the young and the elderly netizens.
12. Deng Aizhu is a retired newspaper editor. She is now in her later seventies.
13. Deng Chang'an is a retired specialist in blood disease at West China Medical College in Chengdu. He is now 83 years old.
14. No, she didn't. She was sitting in her own living room in Beijing chatting face to face with her brother thousands of kilometers away through the Internet.
15. They greeted each other: "Good luck in the Chinese Lunar Monkey Year" through the Internet at the Spring Festival.
16. According to the statistics, there are more than 79 million netizens in China now.
17. Among the more than 79 million netizens in China, some 544,000, or 0.7 per cent of them, are above the age of 60.
18. Dr. Deng enjoys free access to the Internet.
19. Because he can download them from the web and save them on the hard disk.
20. He thinks that the Internet has become a part of his life and work and he would feel very dull without surfing the Internet even for a single day. Yes, it has.

II. **Find the meaning of the words or expressions in Column (A) from those in Column (B).**
   1. H   2. G   3. D   4. J   5. B   6. A   7. E   8. C   9. F   10. I

III. **Fill in the blanks with the words from the blocks, and be sure to use appropriate verb forms and appropriate singular or plural forms for nouns.**
   1. digital, digit
   2. complaining, complaints
   3. surfer, surfing
   4. society, social
   5. upload, download

IV. **Complete the sentences with the given expressions, and change the forms where necessary.**
   1. keep up with
   2. on the other hand
   3. are... inferior to
   4. click onto the net
   5. access to
   6. logs onto
   7. To my astonishment
   8. is engaged in
   9. open... to
   10. stop by

Exercises for Language Structure

I. **Fill in the blanks with proper prepositions.**
   1. through   2. of   3. to   4. from   5. by
   6. into   7. unlike   8. across   9. with   10. without

II. **Choose the best answer.**
   1. D   2. B   3. D   4. D   5. D   6. C   7. C   8. D   9. C   10. B

III. **Find out which of the underlined parts in each sentence is not correct in written English.**
   1. D. except 改为 except when
   2. C. After 改为 In
   3. C. in which 改为 to which
   4. A. As 改为 Like
   5. C. besides 改为 except
   6. D. to ask 改为 on asking
   7. D. belong to 改为 belong
   8. B. with 改为 of
   9. D. of 删除
   10. A. at 改为 from

Practice and Improvement

Reading Skills

Speed Reading I
1. C   2. C   3. B   4. C   5. C   6. F   7. F   8. T   9. T   10. F

Speed Reading II
1. B   2. A   3. D   4. D   5. D   6. F   7. T   8. F   9. T   10. F

Cloze Procedure
1. C   2. B   3. A   4. D   5. C   6. B   7. D   8. C   9. B   10. A

Communication Function

An Interview with a Foreign Boss

A: May I have your name, please?

B: Sure. My name is Zhang Yang, and I've got an English name too. It's Mary.

A: Oh, that's a beautiful name.

B: Thank you.

A: Well, where are you from, Miss Zhang?

B: Oh, I am from Changsha, the capital of Hunan Province.

A: What qualifications do you have that make you think you will be successful in our travel agency?

B: First I have got a diploma in tourism. I finished all the related courses in the Polytechnic with excellent scores.

A: Okay, I see. What are the courses you like best?

B: Oh, English and computer. When I was a sophomore, I earned the Certificate of College Practical English Test A. I'm very good at reading and writing in English. I'm sure my spoken English will be quickly improved if I work in an English-speaking environment. Besides, my communication skills are satisfactory too. Last year I signed up for an English seminar and have benefited from that to a great extent.

A: Have you ever learned how to operate the office equipment?

B: No problem. As you can see from my resume, I've got the Certificate of Computer Practical Competent Test 2. In fact, I'm good at word processing and can type about 80 words per minute.

A: Good. Can you tell me about your work experience, Miss Zhang?

B: Certainly. Last year, I got a part-time job in Hunan Youth Travel Agency as a tourist guide. I have taken several tourist groups to various scenic spots and historical sites. If you take my part-time jobs into account, you'll be more convinced by my experience.

A: Okay. I'm quite satisfied with you. Please wait for our further notice.
B: Thank you. See you later.
A: Good-bye.

Listening Comprehension

I. 1. B   2. D   3. A   4. C   5. A   6. B   7. C   8. A   9. D   10. B

II. 1. A   2. D   3. B   4. A   5. D   6. B   7. D   8. B   9. A   10. A

III. 1. elderly people   2. the Internet
     3. In response to   4. specially designed
     5. website   6. senior Internet lovers
     7. practical programs   8. off line
     9. to compare notes   10. each other

Translation Skills

I. Translate the following into English.

1. Do you often click onto the net and make use of the learning resources on the web?
2. The Internet enables me to maintain ties with the outside world.
3. At the urging of his friends, he took the advice at last.
4. To my astonishment, he even didn't know this matter.
5. I'm afraid Dr. Green is engaged in developing the new product.

II. Translate the following into Chinese.

1. 他有必要通过因特网更新自己的知识。
2. 老师的课非常有趣,班上的学员都全神贯注。
3. 邓医生感到自豪的是他的学生感到他并没有落在时代之后。
4. 学校网吧尤其对那些家人在异国的学生很有帮助。
5. 随着信息技术的发展,对老少网民来说,因特网正变得越来越重要。

Writing Skills

I. Rewrite each of the sentences after the models.

Model A:

1. In spite of his intelligence, he can't work out the difficult problem.
2. Despite their different opinions, they remained good friends.

3. In spite of the heavy rain, they still worked in the field.

4. Despite some faults, he is still popular among the mass.

5. In spite of the darkness outside, the soldiers still set off for the front.

Model B:

1. You can't learn English well without watching out for its idiomatic usage.

2. Plants and animals couldn't live without water or sunlight.

3. You can't hope to spell the words right without paying attention to their pronunciation.

4. I have also learned to absorb the whole sentences without trying to translate them word for word into Chinese.

5. Martin left the house without singing any songs for the rich lady and her guests.

II. Practical Writing

RESUME

Miss Zhang Huixiu

176 Yuhua Avenue, Changsha

Hunan, 420008

Telephone: (0731)2821736

Objective:	To serve a foreign travel agency as a tourist guide
Qualification:	College education with practical experience as a tourist guide, using computer and English skillfully, possessing word-processing ability
Education:	2003–2005 Department of Economic Management, Hunan Polytechnic of Network Engineering, Tourism
	1999–2002 No.21 Middle School, Changsha, Hunan
Experience:	2004 –Present part-time tourist guide in Hunan Youth Travel Agency
Skills:	College English Application Level A, typing 80 wpm
Honors:	Scholarship from President of Hunan Polytechnic of Network Engineering 2003–2004
	"Three–Excellent Student" 2002–2003
Personals:	May 8, 1984, Single, Female, 165cm, 55kg, Excellent health

Tape Scripts for Listening Comprehension

I. Directions: *In this section you will hear 10 statements. Each statement will be read only once. Then there will be a pause. During the pause, you must read the four choices marked A, B, C and D, and decide which is closest in meaning to the sentence you have just heard, and then choose the corresponding letter.*

1. Can I help you?
2. All the boys are not invited to the party.
3. I don't remember calling him.
4. Mrs. Jones is out for tea.
5. We left on our bicycles before dawn.
6. Billy is cleverer than Peter and as intelligent as Carol.
7. I visited Janet before going shopping.
8. Make yourself at home.
9. They hoped she would soon recover from the operation.
10. Come tomorrow unless it rains.

II. Directions: *In this section, you will hear 10 short conversations. At the end of each conversation, a question will be asked about what was said. The conversation and the question will be spoken only once. After each question there will be a pause. During the pause, you must read the four choices marked A, B, C and D, and decide which the best answer is, and then choose the corresponding letter.*

1. M: What can I do for you?
   W: I'd like to have some potatoes, a pound of butter and some vegetables.
   Q: Where does the conversation most probably take place?
2. W: Your radio can't work now. Did you repair it yourself?
   M: Of course not. I asked my brother to do it.
   Q: What does the man say about his radio?
3. M: Jim won't come today. His car broke down last night.
   W: It's too bad. We have to start without him.
   Q: What happened to Jim last night?
4. W: Did you ever play basketball, John?
   M: Oh, yes. I used to play it a long time ago, but now I don't.
   Q: What do we learn from the conversation?
5. M: I saw a girl break our window.
   W: Sorry, Bob. It was me.
   Q: Who broke the window?

6. W: It is raining now. What shall we do then?
   M: It doesn't matter. Let's go into the bar.
   Q: Why do they go into the bar?

7. M: What would you like to have?
   W: I'll try a sandwich and a cup of milk.
   Q: What is the woman going to have?

8. W: Are you doing anything tonight, Bill?
   M: Yes, I have some letters to type for my boss.
   Q: What is the man going to do tonight?

9. M: There will be a new film on at the campus cinema tonight. Would you like to go with me?
   W: I'd love to, but I haven't finished my work yet.
   Q: What does the woman mean?

10. W: Did the flight for New York leave 10 minutes ago?
    M: Yes, it is ten past five now.
    Q: When did the plane take off?

III. Directions: *In this section you will hear a passage of about 90 words three times. There are about 20 words missing. First, you will hear the whole passage from the beginning to the end just to get a general idea about it. Then, in the second reading, write down the missing words during the pauses. You can check what you have written when the passage is read to you once again without the pauses.*

For most **elderly people** who have not had a chance to learn how to use computers, learning about **the Internet** and its use seems terribly challenging. **In response to** this situation, some websites **specially designed** for the elderly have sprung up in recent years.

Established three years ago, the Shanghai-based "Old-Kids" **website** is now well-known among **senior Internet lovers**. They applaud its **practical programs** both online and **off line**. The elderly fans in Shanghai gather in the web's salon **to compare notes** and learn from **each other**.

Online Resources:

1. http://www.iol.co.za/index.php?set_id=1&click_id=31&art_id=qw112489722140B215
2. http://english.people.com.cn/200508/05/eng20050805_200547.html
3. http://www.wpherald.com/storyview.php?StoryID=20050826-032323-7131r
4. http://www.santacruzsentinel.com/archive/2005/August/24/local/stories/07local.htm
5. http://www.messenger-index.com/articles/2005/08/25/news/schhydeclasses.txt

Text Translation for Reference

第七单元　与你息息相关的因特网

A 课文

学校网吧

据报道,美国的许多高中都开设了网吧。现在很多美国高中都对他们的学生开放这些计算机中心。举例来说,马里兰州的一所高中去年三月就开始经营一所网吧。B-CC 高级中学的所有学生都能去这个网吧,学校官员说这个网吧对那些家中没有计算机或在家中不能上网的学生帮助格外大。

这位官员说,该校 13% 的学生来自于贫困家庭,有不少学生是刚从其他国家来到美国。该校学习英语课程的学生说着 23 种不同的语言。

B-CC 高级中学建网吧这一想法开始于 3 年前。那时学校官员正计划重建学校的大楼,而那些对应用技术感兴趣的家长提出建一个网吧。

尽管这个地区的学校已经遭受到了财政预算的削减,但他们还是想要建这个计算机中心。社区也想给予帮助,想要所有的学生都有最好的学习机会。

地区官员赞成这个主意,一个称为 B-CC 高级中学教育基金会的组织也赞成这个主意。这个基金会包括家长、老师、已毕业的学生、企业、社区和其他领导。

两年后,这个基金会筹集到了建立网吧和购置新电脑的资金,它筹集到的钱超过了 17 万美元。现在网吧有 16 台计算机、一台打印机和一个扫描仪。学校官员 Ann Hengerer 说,学生使用互联网获取他们所需要的信息,他们还在计算机上写作业和论文。另外,他们能收发电子邮件,这对那些家人在国外的学生来说尤其有帮助。在网吧,老师们能进行教学研究,还能指导学生如何在互联网上利用教学资源。教师们还把他们的电子教案和网络课件上载到学校网站供学生课后复习。

学校网吧也可为社会提供服务,来访者可在网吧停留,喝杯咖啡、茶或是热巧克力。一位在校生说他们甚至在离校前就可以开始写家庭作业了。

B 课文

老年人上网冲浪

随着信息技术的不断发展,互联网不仅在年轻网民中变得越来越重要,在年纪稍长的网民中,也同样如此。

邓爱珠已经是一位七十高龄的退休报社编辑,最近,她在两年后第一次见到了她惟一的哥哥——一位退休的血液疾病专家。她没有乘坐火车或飞机去她哥哥邓长安住的城市——中国西南的省会城市四川成都。

春节这一天，北京的邓女士坐在客厅里面对面地和她千里之外的哥哥聊天。他们互相问候："猴年大吉！"这是邓女士最近才开始开发的互联网的一个新的方面。

如今像邓女士和她哥哥这样的中国老年人上网的数量正在不断增加。根据中国互联网网络信息中心的数据，在中国7900多万的网民中，大约54.4万或总人数的0.7%的网民的年龄是在60岁以上。虽然人数不多，但他们觉得回报颇丰。

几个月前，在哥哥的催促下，邓女士在计算机上安装了数码摄像头并开始进入雅虎网站进行网上聊天。

邓女士说："能在网上看到我的哥哥，甭提有多高兴了。令人吃惊的是，他看上去健康极了。"

在此之前，她非常担心哥哥的身体状况。

邓大夫83岁时，刚从一次车祸的伤痛中恢复过来。

邓女士说："当我看到他拄着拐杖走路时，我就真正地放心了。"

邓女士从她哥哥那里学到了很多有关计算机的知识，邓大夫每天早餐后就登入互联网，他尤为高兴的是互联网能让他跟上医学的最新发展。

邓大夫说："过去我们西部的医生和沿海的同行比起来常常觉得稍逊一筹，因为他们有更多的机会跟上世界医学的发展。"

"但是现在有很多专门的医疗网站，已经弥补了这个差距，并带给我们这个领域最新的信息。"邓大夫说。

邓女士说："尽管他年岁已高，他仍然每天在互联网上浏览，以跟上他的研究领域的发展并获取最新的消息。他饶有兴趣地探究出现在网上的一切新鲜小发明。"

检查和发送电子邮件已经成为她生活中不可缺少的一部分。她的亲戚、同事和朋友遍布世界各地，而电子邮件将邓女士和他们所有人的距离拉得更近了。

她说："退休生活并没有使我沮丧，因为互联网让我有可能和我周围的世界保持联系。"

她说："通过互联网，我可以看到住在大洋彼岸加利福尼亚的惟一女儿和可爱的外孙，这非常的方便。"

像大多数退休的老人一样，邓女士用钱非常节省，虽然上网比过去要便宜很多，但她仍然认为对于那些退休金是惟一收入来源的老人来说，上网还是有点贵。

另一方面她的哥哥邓大夫却能享受每天24小时的免费上网，因为他仍在华西医学院任教。邓大夫清楚地意识到他需要在这个领域中不断更新自己的知识。他说："如果我仅仅教给学生我几十年前所掌握的陈旧的知识和技术，他们会抱怨的。"

尽管年事已高，邓大夫像大多数退休教授一样，仍然在华西医学院授课。对他来说，通过互联网更新知识是非常必要的。邓大夫说搜索网站其实非常简单，老年人不应该被这些技术所吓倒。

他说："无论你想要知道什么，它就马上会在你眼前出现，你所要做的就是点击正确的链接。"

令邓大夫非常自豪的是，他的学生并没有感到他已落伍。他用微软公司幻灯片软件Power-er Point制作的教案授课，并向学生提供最新出版的医学图表的复印件。这些都是他从网上复制下来,并保存在计算机的硬盘里的。

他补充说:"互联网已成了我生活和工作的一部分,如果一天不上网冲浪,我就会感到非常枯燥。"

Unit Eight

INTERNATIONAL TRADE

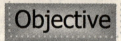

By the end of this unit, the learners are required to grasp the following:

I. Key Words and Phrases

1. Words:

balance	benefit	comparative	consumer	lead
relate	resource	result	specialize	vital

2. Phrases:

adapt... to	be related to	come into being	concentrate on
drain away	due to	exchange...for	in the long run
specialize in	sum up		

II. Language Structure

The Passive Voice

III. Practice and Improvement

Reading Skills: Speed Reading and Cloze Procedure
Speaking Skills: Meeting a Foreign Guest at the Airport
Listening Skills: Sound Recognition, Dialogues, and Spot Dictation
Translation Skills: Phrases and the Passive Voice
Writing Skills: Sentence Patterns and Welcoming Speech

Word Usage

Reading Selection

Text A

1) It has existed in every society, every part of the world, and in fact every day since a primitive man **exchanged** an animal skin for a stone chisel.

   exchange *v. & n.*   to give / giving something to someone and receive something from them   交换,交流,交易

   e.g. He wanted to exchange the foreign money for Renminbi.
   他想把外币兑成人民币。
   He gave me an apple in exchange for a cake.
   他给我一个苹果,换一块蛋糕。
   Let's have an exchange of views on the matter.
   我们就这件事交换一下意见吧。

2) China was among the first to **trade with** other countries.

   trade with   to buy and sell goods or services, especially between countries   同……贸易

   e.g. England trades with nearly all the countries in the world.
   英格兰和几乎全球所有的国家做贸易。
   I refused to trade with that company again.
   我拒绝再和那家公司做生意。

3) In those days goods were moved at great risk and the long journey could get them **considerable** profits because of the scarcity.

   considerable *adj.*   large or of noticeable importance   相当大(或多)的,重要的

   e.g. The fire caused considerable damage to the church.
   这场火给教堂带来了很大的破坏。
   The TV play received considerable acclaim.
   这部电视剧获得很高评价。

4) The Middle Ages saw a boost in the activity of trading as the merchants and producers began **specializing in** making and selling goods and shops appeared in growing numbers.

   specialize in   to spend most of your time studying one particular subject or doing one type of business   专攻,专门研究

   e.g. Tom specialized in chemistry.
   汤姆研究化学。

What did you specialize in?
你主修什么？
She's hired a lawyer who specializes in divorce cases.
她请了一名律师专门负责离婚案件。

5) As the new century progressed, many standard rules and practices **came into being** in order to meet the challenge.
   come into being 形成，产生
   e.g. Before the railway came up into being, a four-horse coach was a popular means of transportation.
   在铁路还没出现以前，四匹马拉的大马车是流行的交通工具。
   This world came into being long ago.
   很久以前就有了世界。

6) Not only are the goods of his own nation available to him, but those of other nations **as well**.
   as well 也，又，同样
   e.g. If you have no pen, a pencil will do as well.
   如果你没有钢笔，铅笔也行。
   Yvonne is learning French and English as well.
   伊冯在学法语，也在学英语。

7) The need to acquire natural resources or capital equipment is **vital** to the well-being of all nations.
   vital *adj.* necessary for the success or continued existence of something; extremely important 生死攸关的，重大的，必需的
   e.g. It is absolutely vital that food supplies should be maintained.
   维持食物的供给是绝对必要的。
   His support is vital for our project.
   他的支援对我们的计划是不可或缺的。

8) Every country in the world will gain by specializing in selling those goods either in which it is absolutely best fit to sell, or at least in which it has **comparative** economic advantages over other countries.
   comparative *adj.* comparing different things 比较的，相当的
   e.g. She's carrying out a comparative study of health in inner cities and rural areas.
   她正在对城市和乡村的健康进行比较研究。
   "Longer" is the comparative form of "long."
   "Longer"是"long"的比较级形式。

9) Some other advantages of exporting as a national objective are its contribution to better use of national resources, ...increasing foreign exchange earnings and improving the **balance of payment**.

balance of payment   the difference between the money that a country receives from exports and the money that it spends on imports   收支差额

balance
① *n.*   天平;平衡;结存
② *v.*   平衡;称;权衡;对比

e.g.   If you earn £100 and spend £60, your balance is £40.
如果你挣 100 镑,花掉 60 镑,那么结余是 40 镑。
The child couldn't keep his balance on his new bicycle.
孩子骑在他的新自行车上不能保持平衡。
The balance of the wages was devoted to new books on flower culture.
剩下来的工资全用来购买有关花卉栽培的新书上了。
Can you balance yourself on skates?
你穿冰鞋能保持平衡吗?
The dancer could balance on one toe.
舞蹈演员可以用一个脚趾平衡。
My accounts balance for the first time this year.
我的账上今年第一次出现收支平衡。

10) Many developing countries continue to **concentrate on** their traditional export products even when the demand for at least some of these products in world markets is decreasing.

concentrate   *v.*   come together, give attention   集中,全神贯注于
concentrate on   集中,全神贯注于

e.g.   Most of the country's population is concentrated in the north.
这个国家的大多数人口都集中在北部。
We concentrated our forces against the enemy's position.
我们集中兵力攻击敌人的阵地。
He is a boy with little power of concentration.
他是个注意力不易集中的男孩。
This thesis will need all your concentration.
这篇论文需要全神贯注才能读懂。
I'm going to concentrate on my writing for a while.
我要集中精力写一会儿。
You should concentrate on your work.
你应该专心于你的工作。
The company is concentrating (its resources) on developing new products.
这家公司集中资源开发新产品。

11) The balance of payments **is not concerned with** movement of money inside a country.

be concerned with 牵涉到，与……有关，参与

e.g. *I am not concerned with that matter any longer.*
我与那事再也没有关系了。

His work is concerned with the preparation of documents for export.
他的工作是准备出口单据。

Outline:

I. (Para. 1–2) Introduction—The History of Trade

  1. It has existed since a primitive man exchanged an animal skin for a stone chisel. (Para. 1)
  2. The Middle Ages saw a boost in the activity of trading. (Para. 2)

II. (Para. 3) The Definition of Exporting

III. (Para. 4–10) The Advantages of Exporting

  1. Exporting will gain by specializing in selling the goods. (Para. 4)
  2. A major benefit of exporting is an increasing opportunity to exploit the comparative advantages. (Para. 5)
  3. Some other advantages of exporting are described one by one in detail. (Para. 6–10)

Text B

1) Otherwise the resources of the company **will be drained away**.

drain away If energy, color, excitement, etc. drains away, it disappears completely, and if something drains it away, it completely removes it. 渐渐枯竭，放干

e.g. *We must dig a trench to drain away the water.*
我们必须挖一条沟排水。

We have to put in another pipe to let the water drain away.
我们得再安一根管道来排水。

2) The golden rule is that **in the medium and the long run** the revenues must exceed the costs in order to sustain the company in existence.

in the medium and the long run 从中长期看

in the long run at a time that is far away in the future 从长期看

in the medium run 从中期看

e.g. *It'll be cheaper in the long run to build it in stone.*
用石头建造从长远看是比较便宜的。

In the long run, receiving a good education is very important.
从长远来看，接受良好的教育是非常重要的。

In the long run, it is an economy to buy good quality goods.
从长远来看,买质量好的物品还是合算的。

3) Different costs **involved in** stages of exporting are likely to be quite considerable, and they are incurred in the expectation of producing revenues.

be involved in   涉及,牵涉,被卷入

e.g. *He was involved in trouble/ disaster.*
他被卷入纠纷/陷入了不幸。

He was involved in working out a plan.
他专心致志地制订计划。

4) However, the market may reject the goods, and the product may be produced too late **due to** changing tastes and circumstances, or the target market may be the wrong one.

due to   owed as a debt or as a right   由于,应归于

e.g. *He made a mistake due to carelessness.*
他由于粗心而犯了个错误。

His illness was due to overwork.
他的病是由于工作过度。

Respect is due to teachers.
教师应受尊敬。

His success was due to hard work.
他的成功都归功于他的努力。

5) **To sum up**, export is vital to the modern society.

sum up   概括,总之

e.g. *The contents of the article may be summed up in a few words.*
这篇文章的内容可以用几句话加以概括。

He summed up to everyone's satisfaction.
他做的总结人人满意。

It sums up in exactly three sentences.
这件事概括起来恰好就是三句话。

Outline:

I. **(Para. 1) Introduction**

Export generates great benefits, but it also involves risks as well.

II. **(Para. 2-5) Benefits and Risks of Export**

1. The final goal of export is the earning of profit. (Para. 2)
2. Export involves risks. (Para. 3-5)

III. (Para. 6) Conclusion

Export is vital to the modern society.

Key to Unit 8

Exercises for Reading Comprehension

I. Answer the following questions.

1. Trade is the exchange of goods and services, and it is one of the most basic activities of mankind.
2. China was among the first to do business with foreign countries. It started trading with the West along the Silk Road from ancient capital Chang'an to Western countries such as Egypt, Rome and some European countries. The fact shows that ancient China played a very important role in promoting the world trade. The products traded were mainly silk products, spices, jewelry, etc.
3. As the wheeled transport means were not available in the ancient time, traders could only use camels, donkeys, horses or other kinds of animals to carry the goods from place to place. The ancient Chinese used camels to cross the desert to the West, which became the most popular means of ancient transport.
4. Business activity boosted during the Middle Age, and modern business came into being since that time.
5. The name of Industrial Revolution was given by economic historians to the period of great changes in economic and social organization that took place, first in Britain (from 1750 to 1850), and later in some countries on the European continent (from 1830), and in USA (from 1860), Japan (from 1870) and Russia (from 1890). During that period the domestic system was replaced by a factory system. It began in Britain with the invention of many kinds of machines, the introduction of steam-power, the division of labor, and the development of road, rail and canal transport.
6. Exporting means the goods are sent and sold out of the country as an act of trade. It is an extension of trade with the customer living in another country.
7. The major benefits of exporting are: it makes better use of national resources; it leads to improvement on the level of technological advance; it reduces unemployment in the country if exporting is related to labor-intensive industries; it obtains foreign exchange required by the exporting country; it keeps the balance of international payments.
8. Open door policy proves to be a right policy. Since this policy was brought into use, many foreign investors and businessmen came to China to trade with us; many joint ventures were set up; all these help promote our exports to other countries.
9. Visible trade is imports and exports in goods; invisible trade is imports and exports in services.

10. Yes, it is. Because we still have something we can't produce to satisfy our own needs. That is why we have to buy some products made in foreign countries. Through the commodity exchange, we can make use of comparative advantage, absorb foreign advanced technology, and improve people's livelihood.
11. Yes, it is extremely important to the modern society.
12. No. The goal of our exporting is not only to earn profit, but profit is essential in comparison with other objectives. How can we venture to export without profit? Under certain circumstance, export serves the interest of foreign affairs, which is one of our trading policies.
13. Yes, it does. Profit depends on two things: the decision makers of a company make the right policy and the sales fleet has thorough knowledge of business experiences.
14. The long-term goal of a company is to make profit; otherwise it can't survive in the competitive market.
15. The revenues must exceed the costs in order to sustain the company in existence.
16. Yes. Risk of failure is always present for all business bodies.
17. Different risks always accompany an exporter. The risks come from the importing country or the customer, the buyer may refuse to pay or to accept the goods; the importing country may have political changes; the shipped goods may be lost or damaged in transit and so on.
18. There are some ways of reducing the risks of exporting, and the most notable one is insurance.
19. Because, by doing so, China can better its people's livelihood and develop its economy.
20. In my opinion, China should speed up its reform and encourage more foreign investors to set up factories and companies in coastal areas, and increase high-tech content to its exports so that its products will be more competitive in the world market.

II. **Find the meaning of the words or expressions in Column (A) from those in Column (B).**
   1. E   2. G   3. D   4. B   5. A   6. J   7. H   8. I   9. C   10. F

III. **Complete the sentences with the given expressions, and change the forms where necessary.**
   1. exchanged... for   2. adapt... to
   3. specializing in   4. came into being
   5. due to   6. in the long run
   7. To sum up   8. concentrate on
   9. be drained away   10. were related to

IV. **Complete the following passage by using appropriate words listed below. Be sure to use singular or plural forms for nouns, and appropriate forms for verbs.**
   1. vital   2. resources
   3. comparative   4. specializing
   5. leads   6. consumers

135

7. benefits
8. results
9. related
10. balance

Exercises for Language Structure

I. Change the following sentences into passive voice.
1. The motor is made to run by electricity.
2. A network center will be built in our college.
3. An expensive birthday present was given by my brother.
4. My report has been proved correct by Prof. Smith.
5. Fuel had been used for thousands of years before the exploitation of oil.
6. Miss Green was offered an important position.
   An important position was offered to Miss Green.
7. The mistake was considered to be very serious.
8. She was made to wait for over an hour in the train because of the delay.
9. The cleaner found the purse which was left in the classroom yesterday.
10. In the future, mails will not be sent to the houses by the deliverers but through the Internet.

II. Fill in the blanks with the correct tense and voice of the given verbs.
1. was destroyed
2. will have been built
3. can be depended on
4. has been sent
5. was praised
6. will be brought
7. had been injured
8. have taken place
9. had been washed, would be set up
10. graduated, would be employed

III. Choose the best answer.
1. A   2. C   3. A   4. B   5. B   6. C   7. B   8. B   9. C   10. A

IV. Find out which of the underlined parts in each sentence is not correct in written English.
1. A. It 改为 It's
2. C. has raised 改为 has been raised
3. B. has been passed 改为 has passed
4. C. was existed 改为 existed
5. C. explained 改为 been explained
6. D. was remained 改为 remained
7. A. should have informed 改为 should have been informed
8. C. must take 改为 (should) be taken
9. C. is covered 改为 are covered

10. B. had damaged 改为 had been damaged

Practice and Improvement

Reading Skills

Speed Reading I
1. C   2. D   3. D   4. A   5. D   6. F   7. T   8. F   9. F   10. F

Speed Reading II
1. C   2. B   3. C   4. B   5. D   6. F   7. F   8. T   9. T   10. T

Cloze Procedure
1. D   2. D   3. D   4. C   5. B   6. C   7. B   8. C   9. C   10. A

Communication Function

Meeting a Foreign Guest at the Railway Station

A: Excuse me, but aren't you Mr. Green from Imperial Trading Company, Liverpool?

B: Yes, I am. Here's my card.

A: I'm from Hunan Embroidery Import & Export Corp. My name is Liu Lan.

B: Glad to meet you, Miss Liu. These are members of my delegation. Let me introduce them to you. This is Mr. Don Bradley, our export manager.

C: Glad to see you, Ms Liu.

B: This is Miss Kate McKenna, my secretary.

D: Nice to see you, Ms Liu.

A: I'm glad to see all of you. Welcome to Changsha.

B: Thank you, Ms Liu. It's very nice of you to come all the way and meet us.

A: It's a pleasure to meet our foreign guests. Did you have a good journey?

B: Yes, I did. Thank you.

A: Anyway it's a long trip and I think you'd better take a rest to recover from weariness. Let's go to the hotel. Our car is waiting out of the railway station.

B: Oh, that's very considerate of you. Let's go.

Listening Comprehension

I. 1. B   2. A   3. A   4. B   5. B   6. B   7. A   8. B   9. A   10. B

II. 1. C   2. B   3. C   4. D   5. A   6. C   7. B   8. B   9. C   10. D

III.
1. on foreign trade
2. to upgrade
3. a manufacturing center
4. less developed countries
5. competitors
6. lose its advantages
7. in the near future
8. higher-end products
9. in exports
10. technologies

Translation Skills

I. **Translate the following into English.**
1. We are a joint venture, specializing in the import and export of silk goods.
2. We must strengthen the development of new products so that our goods can be adapted to the need of customers.
3. Trade came into being since a primitive man exchanged an animal skin for a stone chisel.
4. If a company can't make profits in the medium and the long run, the resources of the company will be drained away.
5. It is vital to a country to keep balance of international payments.

II. **Translate the following into Chinese.**
1. 虽然已经做出了巨大努力,但问题仍然远未解决。
2. 去年外国公司对2/3的高科技专利和发明进行了注册。
3. 众所周知,商品贸易是有形的进出口,而服务贸易是无形的进出口。
4. 据报道,由于采取了得力的措施,非典型性肺炎的蔓延已得到控制。
5. 我们邀请了郝尔先生给我们做一个国际贸易的讲座,但他太忙了,没有接受这一邀请。

Writing Skills

I. **Rewrite the sentences after the models.**

Model A:
1. Close attention should be paid to English idioms if you want to use the language freely.
2. Full preparations have been made for the exam, and Edward is sure that he can succeed in it.
3. Careful researches are being made on solar energy by the experts so as to replace the fuel energy.
4. A solid foundation was laid of mathematics because John was determined to become a mathematician.
5. A leading role is played in the management of the company by Mr. Harris.

Model B:
1. It was said that the castle had been destroyed in the war.
2. It is reported that some new medicines have been developed to cure AIDS.
3. It is known that some precautions have been taken to prevent AIDS.
4. It is believed that the folk song has been collected in this region.

5. It was reported that the foal, Prometea had been cloned by some Italian biologists.

II. Practical Writing

Welcoming Speech

Ladies and Gentlemen,

  This morning we feel very much honored to have a chance of meeting joyfully with Prof. Brown, who is already known to us for his great achievements in research work of international trade and economic development. First of all, please allow me on behalf of all present here to extend our warm welcome and cordial greetings to our distinguished guest who comes from afar.

  Prof. Brown has been engaged in the study of international trade and related subjects for many years, and he has published a number of important academic theses and works. Recently he visited a lot of places, giving many academic lectures on international trade and economic development and winning respectful appreciation of his audiences.

  This morning he is going to address us "International Trade and Economic Globalization."

  Now let us ask Prof. Brown to make a report for us with warm applause.

Tape Scripts for Listening Comprehension

I. Directions: *Listen to the following sentences. Choose which word the speaker on the tape says. Tick the right word.*

1. This has a great **effect** on industry in the developing countries.
2. The **idea** of exporting of nations' surpluses of the products may be accepted by people very easily.
3. Hand **labor** was replaced by machines, and goods could be made in greater quantities in less time and at lower costs than ever before.
4. If imports and exports are not balanced, it is necessary for the government to **correct** the deficit by adjusting the trade policies.
5. Analysts expect that it will be difficult to maintain a high **growth** rate for exports next year.
6. China will **further** open its financial, commercial and tourism industries to foreign investors.
7. The event which most **stimulated** the development of modern trading was the Industrial Revolution.
8. More and more regions are favored by foreign investors **besides** the Yangtze River Delta and the Pearl River Delta.

9. Two thirds of high-tech **patents** and inventions were registered by foreign companies last year.
10. It is foolish to export numerous **socks** and then import one Boeing plane.

II. Directions: *In this section, you will hear 10 short conversations. At the end of each conversation, a question will be asked about what was said. The conversation and the question will be spoken only one time. After each question, there will be a pause. During the pause, you must read the four choices marked A, B, C and D, and decide which the best answer is, and then choose the corresponding letter.*

1. M: I can't understand why my friend isn't here yet. We agreed to meet at 10:30. It's almost 11:00.
   W: She probably just got tied up in the traffic. Let's give her a few more minutes.
   Q: What are these people going to do?

2. M: What did you do yesterday?
   W: I stayed in and did some housework and homework.
   Q: Where was the woman yesterday?

3. M: The train is supposed to leave for New York at 2:30.
   W: 2:30! But it's already three o'clock.
   Q: What does the woman mean?

4. W: Excuse me, would you mind if I use your phone?
   M: Help yourself, it's on the table over there.
   Q: What does the man tell the woman to do?

5. W: I've already received ten Christmas cards.
   M: I've only got half that many. I hope I can have some more today.
   Q: How many Christmas cards have the man received?

6. M: The mountain seems higher. It really makes me dizzy to climb it this year.
   W: The mountain may not be higher, but we're older.
   Q: What has changed since last year?

7. W: The special for today is baked chicken and lettuce.
   M: No, thank you. Just bring me a cup of coffee, please.
   Q: Where does the conversation most probably take place?

8. W: How did Paul do in the swim yesterday?
   M: Well, we had a good start, but he quickly fell behind.
   Q: What does the man mean?

9. W: How much are these jackets?
   M: Five dollars each and nine dollars for two.
   Q: How much does one jacket cost?

10. M: I'm a little tired, so I think I'll go to the students' café and listen to a little music. Care to join me?
    W: I'd love to, but I have to go to the library to look at a book on reserve.
    Q: Why can't the woman go with the man?

III. Directions: *In this section you will hear a passage of about 90 words three times. There are about 20 words missing. First, you will hear the whole passage from the beginning to the end just to get a general idea about it. Then, in the second reading, write down the missing words during the pauses. You can check what you have written when the passage is read to you once again without the pauses.*

Li Yushi, an expert **on foreign trade**, agrees that it is time for China **to upgrade** its exports. He explained that China has been **a manufacturing center** of low-end exports for years and some **less developed countries** are increasingly becoming **competitors** in that sector. "China may **lose its advantages** on low-end products manufacture **in the near future** as its costs grow, and it should move onto **higher-end products**," he said. "China's manufacturers will suffer more **in exports** if they can not master **technologies**," he added.

Online Resources:

1. http://www.etraveldictionary.com/Term.php?term=Export%20%20%20&dictID=7
2. http://www.tdctrade.com/chinastat/img/20MEP.xls
3. http://www.chinadaily.com.cn/english/doc/2005-08-27/content_472769.htm
4. http://au.biz.yahoo.com/050826/17/82bc.html
5. http://www.chinadaily.com.cn/english/doc/2005-08-27/content_472710.htm

Text Translation for Reference

第八单元 国际贸易

A 课文

为什么要出口？

贸易，是商品和服务的交换，是人类最基本的活动之一。贸易存在于每一个社会，存在于世界的每一个角落，实际上，自从原始人用兽皮换取石凿以来，贸易活动每天都存在着。贯穿早期历史，中国是最早与其他国家进行贸易的国家之一。甚至在公元前，就有商人驱赶着长长的骆驼商队沿着丝绸之路，从中国跋涉到西方，然后遍布各地。那时商品运输危险重重，但由于商品的稀奇珍贵，遥远的路途能给商人带来可观的收益。

中世纪期间，随着制造商开始从事专门的生产，商人开始从事专门的销售，于是出现了越来越多的店铺，因而贸易活动迅速发展。对现代贸易发展最具有推动作用的事件便是始于1760年的英国工业革命。机器生产代替了手工操作，因而能比以往任何时候，能在更短的时间内，以更低的成本，生产更多的产品。跨入新世纪之后，许多标准规则和惯例为迎接挑战应运而生。

出口是与另一国家的顾客进行贸易，这是贸易的一种延伸。这种贸易活动的延伸非常重要，它可使买主从多种商品中进行选择，以满足自己的需要。不仅本国的商品可供他挑选，而且其他国家的商品也可供其选择。这种获取自然资源或固定设备的需求对于所有国家的稳定安宁都是非常重要的。

把国家剩余产品进行出口，这一主意能被人们轻易地接受。世界上每个国家都能够通过专门销售这些剩余产品而获利，不管产品是绝对适合出口，还是与其他国家相比，产品至少具有可竞争性的利润优势。这些优势可能包括土壤、矿床、特殊的精神或身体能力，还有地理位置等等。

出口的主要益处之一，就在于它有更多的机会来利用使国内市场上的生产者所享受的比较优势。对于一个国家来说，出口的益处还体现在它能为国家更合理地利用资源、促进科技进步、提高就业率、增加外汇收入以及改善贸易支付差额。

国家资源的更合理利用

不少发展中国家继续集中精力生产他们传统的出口产品，即使这些产品中，某些产品的需求量在世界市场上正在减少。显然，为了其利益，它们应该把资源用在需求量日益增大的产品上。产品和市场的多样化是至关重要的，因为有些发展中国家的传统产品只有有限的增长前景。

科技进步

出口的扩展和多样化同样能导致技术水平的改进。国际市场的竞争促使出口商常常采用更为现代的技术加工和生产方法，来调整自己的产品以适应市场的需要。在发展中国家，这会对工业产生巨大的效果。

就业增加

出口对就业也非常重要，尤其是如果出口产品与劳动密集型产业关系密切，那么，这些地区或国家的就业机会就非常多。自从1978年中国改革开放的政策实施以来，中国建立了很多以出口为主的企业和合资企业，如今的中国已经成为世界制造业中心。不少年轻人已经从农村来到了城市和沿海地区，在这些企业做事，从而减少了就业的压力。

外汇收入

一个国家必须通过出口它在生产中享有优势的产品，才能有外汇盈余，然后用此盈余来进口那些该国不具备比较优势的产品。只有靠出口一部分的工农业产品，我们才有足够的外汇去进口在实现现代化的过程中所必需的技术和设备。

贸易支付差额

贸易支付差额与国内的货币流通无关。它是流入国家的货币数量和流出国家的货币数量之间的差额。人们知道商品贸易是有形的进出口贸易，而劳务进出口则是无形贸易。如果进出口贸易不平衡，政府就有必要通过调整贸易政策来纠正赤字。

B 课文

出口的利润和风险

出口对于现代社会是非常重要的。它能产生巨大的利润,同时也会存在风险。

出口就是为了利润

我们已经引证了从事出口尤其是国际出口具有许多目的性,然而其最终目的就是赚取利润。如果最终目的达不到,那么上述其他目的更无从谈起。出口公司的收益性在很大程度上是依靠管理和专业能力的改进。产品的生产活动、宣传活动以及流通活动涉及大量的费用支出。这些支出必须少于销售所得的收入,否则,公司的资产将会被耗费掉,并将逐渐枯竭,最终破产。因此,一个以出口为主的企业必须密切注视其经营和管理,以确保盈利。有时候,一个公司为了开发新产品,可以承受短期的亏损。然而这些亏损应该是有限度的,而且绝不允许无限期地亏损下去。万全之策就是在中长期内收入必须大于支出,以便公司能持续生存下去。

出口也存在风险

对企业来说,失败的风险总是存在的。各个出口阶段的不同费用可能有很多,产生这些费用是由于期望由此带来收入。然而市场有可能不接受这些产品,也有可能由于口味和环境的改变使得产品生产滞后,或者目标市场是错误的。

因此,由于各种各样的原因致使费用无法弥补,而且,很多企业没有财力来承受多次的失败。至于为顾客提供信贷,顾客可能会有欺诈行为,尤其是某一主要顾客在财务方面的崩溃或许是致命的。

自然灾害和政治剧变的风险也是生意环境的一部分,它们会使生意突然中断和永久中断。很多国家都有减少出口风险的办法,最值得注意的办法就是保险,在学会如何进行贸易的同时我们也必须学会如何避免风险。

总之,出口对于现代社会是很重要的。它能产生巨大的效益,同时也存在着风险。已经证实国民经济在很大程度上受国际贸易的影响。中国为了改善人民的生活必须做好出口贸易,为此目的,我们必须明确为什么要出口以及如何出口这两个问题。这个问题看似简单,但并不是所有人都能明白。

REVISION II

Key to Test Paper 2

Part I. Listening Comprehension (15%)

Section A. (5%)
1. D 2. D 3. C 4. A 5. B 6. A 7. C 8. B 9. A 10. B

Section B. (5%)
11. C 12. A 13. B 14. B 15. C 16. C 17. D 18. B 19. A 20. D

Section C. (5%)
21. factory inventories
22. production needs
23. company payrolls
24. up to date
25. For example
26. what brand of goods
27. through the Internet
28. goods and services
29. through e-commerce
30. costs and inventories

Part II. Grammar and Vocabulary (30%)

Section A. *Fill in the blanks with proper prepositions.* (10%)
31. along 32. into 33. until 34. with 35. through
36. onto 37. from 38. for 39. between 40. by

Section B. *Write the words in the right column according to the meaning in the left column.* (10%)
41. J 42. G 43. H 44. C 45. A 46. D 47. B 48. E 49. F 50. I

Section C. *Choose the best answer.* (10%)
51. A 52. B 53. A 54. C 55. D 56. C 57. B 58. B 59. B 60. D
61. C 62. C 63. A 64. A 65. B 66. B 67. D 68. C 69. C 70. D

Part III. Reading Comprehension (30%)

71. C   72. C   73. D   74. C   75. D   76. A   77. C   78. D
79. C   80. D   81. C   82. B   83. B   84. D   85. D

Part IV. Translation (10%)

86. 她很快地掌握了这项技能,并发现计算机对她学习意大利语课程具有很大价值。
87. 如果我们有更长的时间和更多的电脑和打印机,那么网吧就能为更多的学生服务了。
88. 科技工作者仅用了 18 个月的时间完成了大型分布式平面应用软件系统的开发。
89. 据悉,第一台"银河系 III 型"计算机投入军队使用以来,在军事部署和国防科学研究中发挥了重要的作用。
90. 由于在网上拍卖领域没有经验和工程师,新浪公司相信与雅虎公司的合作将会解决这些问题。

Part V. Practical Writing (15%)

Resume

Zhang Huiling
156 Qingyuan Road, Changsha
Hunan, 410004
Telephone: 0731-5581506

Objective:	To serve a foreign export oriented enterprise as an accountant
Qualification:	College education with practical experience in accounting, knowing Western style accounting well, using computer and English skillfully and possessing word-processing competence
Education:	2002–2005, Department of Finance, Hunan Polytechnic of Commerce, Major: Commercial Accounting
1999–2002, Xiangya Senior Middle School
Experience:	2003–Present, part-time accountant in New World Supermarket
Skills:	2004, Computer Application & Operation, Level 2, typing 60 wpm
Honors:	Scholarship from President of Hunan Polytechnic of Commerce 2003–2004, Three-good student 2002–2004
Personals:	July 6, 1982, Single, Female, 163cm, 55kg, Excellent health

Tape Scripts for Test Paper 2

Part I. Listening Comprehension (15%)

Section A. Directions: *In this section you will hear 10 statements. Each statement will be read only once. Then there will be a pause. During the pause, you must read the four choices marked A, B, C and D, and decide which is closest in meaning to the sentence you have just heard, and then choose the corresponding letter.* (5%)

1. Jim is a doctor like his father's brother.
2. Rose lost four pounds on a diet, but her sister lost twice as much.
3. Although Mary studied hard for the test, there were a lot of questions she couldn't answer.
4. He's been decorating the bathroom, and he's got paint in his hair.
5. They would have fixed the refrigerator yesterday except that it was a holiday.
6. We'll have to leave at nine o'clock in order to get to the office before nine-thirty.
7. Last month was too soon to plant the trees and next month will be too late.
8. Sophia went to the market for some vegetables, but she got some flowers instead.
9. Do you have time to go over the English text with me?
10. Professor Young is trying to set up his own computer company.

Section B. Directions: *In this section, you will hear 10 short conversations. At the end of each conversation, a question will be asked about what was said. The conversation and the question will be spoken only one time. After each question, there will be a pause. During the pause, you must read the four choices marked A, B, C and D, and decide which the best answer is, and then choose the corresponding letter.* (5%)

11. W: If we hurry we can take the subway and save an hour, can't we?
    M: Yes, the subway takes only half an hour to get there.
    Q: How long does it take to get there by subway?
12. W: This is my raincoat.
    M: No, it's Jim's. Yours is at the office.
    Q: Whose raincoat is it?
13. W: What do you think of little Tom?
    M: Well, compared to Billy, he's a genius.
    Q: What does the man think?
14. W: I'm going to the doctor. I have something wrong with my ears.
    M: I never have anything wrong with my ears.
    Q: Where is she going?

15. W: When will my car be fixed?
    M: Well, it's two by my watch. I think you can get it in a couple of hours.
    Q: When can the woman get her car?
16. W: Didn't you tell Tom about the meeting?
    M: Whatever I say to him goes in one ear to the other.
    Q: What does the man mean?
17. W: Hand in your composition before Saturday. I am going to go over it during the weekend.
    M: Sure. I will finish it as soon as possible.
    Q: What is the probable relationship between the two speakers?
18. W: I've brought lunch. We can eat at the park.
    M: That's much more fun than eating at the restaurant.
    Q: Where are they going to eat lunch?
19. M: Your house is bigger than mine.
    W: So is Bob's, but Tom's is smaller.
    Q: Whose house is the smallest?
20. M: Our team won yesterday's football match.
    W: Oh, you're getting better, are you?
    Q: What does the woman mean?

Section C. Directions: *In this section you will hear a passage of about 90 words three times. There are about 20 words missing. First, you will hear the whole passage from the beginning to the end just to get a general idea about it. Then, in the second reading, write down the missing words during the pauses. You can check what you have written when the passage is read to you once again without the pauses.* (5%)

> In business and industry, computers are used to prepare **factory inventories**, keep track of sales trends and **production needs**, mail dividend checks, and make out **company payrolls**. It can also keep bank accounts **up to date** and make out electronic bills. **For example**, they can tell you **what brand of goods** are the most popular in a particular supermarket, and people can do e-shopping at home **through the Internet**. Some multinational corporations, like IBM and Microsoft in America, can provide **goods and services** on demand of the customers **through e-commerce**, thus greatly reducing the **costs and inventories**.

教学大纲与实施方案

（仅供参考）

I. 教学目的和要求

《新世纪英语教程》第二册按照教育部高等教育司《高职高专教育英语课程教学基本要求》编写，要求学生在学习本教材前，应掌握《新世纪英语教程》第一册中所规定的基本的英语语音、词汇和语法知识，在听、说、读、写、译等方面受过基本的训练。

本教材贯彻听说领先的原则，重在培养学生实际使用英语进行交际的能力，同时培养学生较强的阅读能力，并兼顾写作、翻译等各项能力的发展，使学生具备以英语为工具，捕捉和获取所需信息的能力，为学习各种专业英语打下坚实基础。

第二册的编排体例采用主题教学(Theme-based)模式：从不同侧面围绕一个激发学生兴趣和思考的共同主题，把听、说、读、写、译等各种技能的训练合理安排在一个单元内，教学活动以阅读为中心，结合主题预演、课文问答、语言结构、听力理解、交际技巧、翻译训练、应用写作等，从而将教与学有机结合，课内外连成一片，使学生真正做到听得懂、说得出、用得活。

本学期的学习和考试范围为教材的1～8单元。其教学目的是经过教学计划中规定的学时数的教学，使学生掌握一定的英语基础知识，具有一定听、说、读、写、译的语言技能。

具体语言技能的要求

1. 阅读技能
   1) 理解文章的主旨或要点
   2) 理解文章中的具体信息
   3) 根据上下文推断生词意思
   4) 根据上下文做出简单的判断和推理
   5) 理解文章的写作意图、作者的见解和态度等
   6) 就文章内容做出结论
   7) 快速查找有关信息
   8) 对难度稍低于课文、语法结构类似的阅读材料，每分钟阅读速度达到50词，掌握一定速度技巧，快速阅读时达到每分钟60～70词，理解正确率达到70%左右。

2. 说的技能
   1) 模拟或套用常用口头交际句型，就日常生活和有关业务提出问题和简短回答
   2) 交流有困难时能采取简单的应变措施

3. 听的技能
   1) 理解所听材料的主旨或要点
   2) 理解具体信息

3) 理解所听材料的背景、说话人之间的关系等

4) 推断所听材料的含义

4. 翻译(英译汉)技能

1) 正确翻译一般语句,能正确理解本册教材中常用的习语和短语,译文基本符合汉语习惯和语法规范

2) 正确掌握"it"句型的译法

3) 正确掌握直接引语和间接引语的译法

4) 正确掌握虚拟语气的译法

5) 正确掌握倒装句的译法

6) 正确掌握介词短语的译法

7) 正确掌握被动句的译法

5. 写的技能

1) 正确使用所学的词、词组和句型

2) 语法及标点使用正确,句子结构完整

3) 句子意思清楚,符合逻辑顺序

4) 注意连贯性,正确使用连接手段:如 on the one hand ... on the other hand 等

5) 正确套用或使用常见的应用文格式,如信封、信函、公约和守则、海报、广告、成绩通知单、履历和欢迎辞等

II. 教学时间安排

本学期计划用 72 课时学习这门课程,每星期 4 节课。全书共 8 个单元,每个单元学习 8 个课时,期中复习 4 课时,期末复习 4 课时,总计 72 课时。要求每单元的听说课不得少于 2 课时。

内容	时间	课时
1. Unit One	第一周~第二周	8 课时
2. Unit Two	第三周~第四周	8 课时
3. Unit Three	第五周~第六周	8 课时
4. Unit Four	第七周~第八周	8 课时
5. Mid-term Revision	第九周	4 课时
6. Unit Five	第十周~十一周	8 课时
7. Unit Six	十二周~十三周	8 课时
8. Unit Seven	十四周~十五周	8 课时
9. Unit Eight	十六周~十七周	8 课时
10. Terminal Revision	十八周	4 课时

III. 平时作业和期末考试

该课程成绩评定采取平时成绩和期末考试结合的方法,其中平时形成性考核成绩占

30%,期末终结性考试成绩占70%。

平时作业

由任课教师根据学生实际情况与需要布置。

注:作业共10次,其中8个单元8次,期中复习1次,期末复习1次,每次记10分,共100分。

期末考试

本课程的期末考试为闭卷考试,满分为100分。考试题型如下:

序号	测试项目	题号	测试内容	题型	百分比	时间分配
I	听力理解	1~15	句子、对话、短文	多项选择、填空	15%	15分钟
II	语法结构和词汇	16~35	词法、词形变化等	多项选择、填空	15%	15分钟
III	阅读理解	36~60	语篇,包括一般性及应用性文字	多项选择、填空、简答、匹配	35%	40分钟
IV	英译汉	61~65	句子和段落	句子(多项选择)、段落翻译	20%	25分钟
V	写作/汉译英		应用文(启事、通知、请柬、名片、明信片、电子邮件等)或实用性段落/短文翻译	套写、书写、填写或翻译	15%	25分钟
	合计	65+1			100%	120分钟